SHAKESPEARE

THE TEMPEST

NOTES

COLES EDITORIAL BOARD

Bound to stay open

Publisher's Note

Otabind (Ota-bind). This book has been bound using the patented Otabind process. You can open this book at any page, gently run your finger down the spine, and the pages will lie flat.

ABOUT COLES NOTES

COLES NOTES have been an indispensible aid to students on five continents since 1948.

COLES NOTES are available for a wide range of individual literary works. Clear, concise explanations and insights are provided along with interesting interpretations and evaluations.

Proper use of COLES NOTES will allow the student to pay greater attention to lectures and spend less time taking notes. This will result in a broader understanding of the work being studied and will free the student for increased participation in discussions.

COLES NOTES are an invaluable aid for review and exam preparation as well as an invitation to explore different interpretive paths.

COLES NOTES are written by experts in their fields. It should be noted that any literary judgement expressed herein is just that – the judgement of one school of thought. Interpretations that diverge from, or totally disagree with any criticism may be equally valid.

COLES NOTES are designed to supplement the text and are not intended as a substitute for reading the text itself. Use of the NOTES will serve not only to clarify the work being studied, but should enhance the readers enjoyment of the topic.

ISBN 0-7740-3801-2

© COPYRIGHT 2005 AND PUBLISHED BY
COLES PUBLISHING COMPANY
TORONTO - CANADA
PRINTED IN CANADA

Manufactured by Webcom Limited
Cover finish: Webcom's Exclusive **DURACOAT**

CONTENTS

WILLIAM SHAKESPEARE: LIFE AND WORKS
Biographical Sketch

The Early Years

Despite the scholarship it has generated, our knowledge of Shakespeare's life is sketchy, filled with more questions than answers, even after we discard the misinformation accumulated over the years. He was baptized on April 26, 1564, in Holy Trinity Church, Stratford-on-Avon. As it was customary to baptize children a few days after birth, he was probably born on April 23. The monument erected in Stratford states that he died on April 23, 1616, in his fifty-third year.

William was the third child of John Shakespeare, who came to Stratford from Snitterfield before 1532 as a "whyttawer" (tanner) and glover, and Mary Arden, daughter of a wealthy "gentleman of worship" from Wilmecote. They married around 1557. Since John Shakespeare owned one house on Greenhill Street and two on Henley Street, we cannot be certain where William was born, though the Henley Street shrine draws many tourists each year. William's two older sisters died in infancy, but three brothers and two other sisters survived at least into childhood.

Shakespeare's father was well-to-do, dealing in farm products and wool, and owning considerable property in Stratford. After holding a series of minor municipal offices he was elected alderman in 1565, high bailiff (roughly similar to the mayor of today) in 1568, and chief alderman in 1571. There are no records of young Will Shakespeare's education (though there are many unfounded legends), but he probably attended the town school maintained by the burgesses, which prepared its students for the universities. Ben Jonson's line about Shakespeare's having "small *Latine*, and lesse *Greeke*" refers not to his education but to his lack of indebtedness to the classical writers and dramatists.

On November 27, 1582, a licence to marry was issued to "Willelmum Shaxpere *et* Annam Whateley *de* Temple Grafton." On the next day a marriage bond for "Willm Shagspere" and "Anne Hathwey of Stratford" was signed by Fulk Sandells and John Richardson, farmers of Stratford. This bond stated that there was no "lawful let or impediment by reason of any precontract, consanguinity, affinity, or by any other lawful means whatsoever"; thus "William and Anne (were) to be married together with once asking of the banns of matrimony." The problem of Anne Whateley has led many researchers to argue all kinds of improbabilities, such as the existence of two different Shakespeares and the forging of documents to conceal Shakespeare's true identity. The actual explanation seems to be simple: the clerk who

1

made the marriage licence entry apparently copied the name "Whateley" from a preceding entry, as a glance at the full sheet suggests. (Incidentally, Nicholas Rowe in his life of Shakespeare, published in 1709, well before the discovery of these marriage records, gave Anne's name as Hathaway.) The problems of marriage with Anne Hathaway — he was eighteen and she was twenty-six — and of the bond have caused similar consternation. Why did these two marry when there was such a discrepancy of age? Why only one saying of the banns (rather than the usual three)? Why the emphasis on a possible legal problem? The answer here is not simple or definite, but the birth of a daughter Susanna, baptized at Holy Trinity on May 26, 1583, seems to explain the odd circumstances. It should be recognized, however, that an engagement to marry was considered legally binding in those days (we still have breach-of-promise suits today) and that premarital relations were not unusual or frowned upon when an engagement had taken place. The circumstances already mentioned, Shakespeare's ensuing activities, and his will bequeathing to Anne "my second best bed with the furniture" have suggested to some that their marriage was not entirely happy. Their other children, the twins Hamnet and Judith, were christened on February 2, 1585.

Theatrical Life

Shakespeare's years before and immediately after the time of his marriage are not charted, but rumor has him as an apprentice to a master butcher or as a country teacher or an actor with some provincial company. He is supposed to have run away from whatever he was doing for livelihood and to have gone to London, where he soon joined a theatrical group. At this time there were only two professional houses established in London, The Theatre (opened in 1576) and The Curtain (opened in 1577). His first connection with the theater was reputedly as holder of horses; that is, one of the stage crew, but a most inferior assignment. Thereafter he became an actor (perhaps at this time he met Ben Johnson), a writer, and a director. Such experience had its mark in the theatricality of his plays. We do know that he was established in London by 1592, when Robert Greene lamented in *A Groatsworth of Wit* (September, 1592) that professional actors had gained priority in the theater over university-trained writers like himself: "There is an upstart Crow, beautified with our feathers, that with his *Tygers hart wrapt in a Players hyde,* supposes he is as well able to bombast out a lanke verse as the best of you: and beeing an absolute *Iohannes fac totum* (Jack-of-all-trades), is in his owne conceit the onely Shake-scene in a countrey." An apology for Greene's ill-humored statement by Henry Chettle, the editor of the pamphlet, appeared around December 1592 in *Kind-Hart's Dream.*

Family Affairs

To return to the known details of his family life, Shakespeare's

2

son Hamnet was buried at Stratford on August 11, 1596; his father was given a coat of arms on October 20, 1596; and Will purchased New Place (a refurbished tourist attraction today) on May 4, 1597. The London playwright obviously had not severed connections with his birthplace, and he was reflecting his new affluence by being known as William Shakespeare of Stratford-upon-Avon, in the County of Warwick, Gentleman. His father was buried in Stratford on September 8, 1601; his mother, on September 9, 1608. His daughter Susanna married Dr. John Hall on June 5, 1607, and they had a child named Elizabeth. His other daughter, Judith, married Thomas Quiney on February 10, 1616, without special licence, during Lent and was thus excommunicated. Shakespeare revised his will on March 25, 1616, and was buried on April 25, 1616 (according to the parish register). A monument by Gerard Janssen was erected in the Holy Trinity chancel in 1623 but many, like Milton several years later, protested:

What needs my *Shakespeare* for his honour'd Bones,
The labour of an age in piled Stone, . . .
Thou in our wonder and astonishment
Hast built thy self a live-long Monument.

Shakespeare's Writings

Order of Appearance
Dating of Shakespeare's early plays, while based on inconclusive evidence, has tended to hover around the early 1590s. Almost certainly, it is his chronicles of Henry the Sixth that Philip Henslowe, an important theatrical manager of the day, referred to in his diary as being performed during March-May, 1592. An allusion to these plays also occurs in Thomas Nashe's *Piers Penniless His Supplication to the Devil* (August, 1592).

The first published work to come from Shakespeare's hand was *Venus and Adonis* (1593), a long poem, dedicated to Henry Wriothesley, Earl of Southampton. A year later *The Rape of Lucrece* appeared, also dedicated to Southampton. Perhaps poetry was pursued during these years because the London theaters were closed as a result of an outbreak of plague. The *Sonnets*, published in 1609, may owe something to Southampton, who had become Shakespeare's patron. Perhaps some were written as early as the first few years of the 1590's. They were mentioned (along with a number of plays) in 1598 by Francis Meres in his *Palladis Tamia*, and sonnets 138 and 144 were printed without authority by William Jaggard in *The Passionate Pilgrim* (1599).

There is a record of a performance of *A Comedy of Errors* at Gray's Inn (one of the law colleges) on December 28, 1594, and, during early 1595, Shakespeare was paid, along with the famous actors Richard Burbage and William Kempe, for performances before the Queen by the Lord Chamberlain's Men, a theatrical company formed the year before. The company founded the Globe Theatre in 1599 and became the King's Men when James ascended the throne. Records show frequent payments to the company through its general manager John Heminge. From 1595 through 1614 there are numerous references to real estate transactions and other legal matters, to many performances, and to various publications connected with Shakespeare.

Order of Publication

The first plays to be printed were *Titus Andronicus* around February, 1594, and the garbled versions of *Henry VI*, Parts II and III in 1594. Thereafter *Richard III* appeared in 1597 and 1598; *Richard II*, in 1597 and twice in 1958; *Romeo and Juliet*, in 1597 (a pirated edition) and 1599, and many others. Some of the plays appear in individual editions, with or without Shakespeare's name on the title page, but eighteen are known only from their appearance in the first collected volume (the so-called First Folio) of 1623. The editors were Heminge and Henry Condell, another member of Shakespeare's company. *Pericles* was omitted from the First Folio although it had appeared in 1609, 1611, and 1619; it was added to the Third Folio in 1664.

There was reluctance to publish plays at this time for various reasons; many plays were carelessly written for fast production; collaboration was frequent; plays were not really considered *reading* matter; they were sometimes circulated in manuscript; and the theatrical company, not the author, owned the rights. Those plays given individual publication appeared in a quarto, so named from the size of the page. A single sheet of paper was folded twice to make four leaves (thus *quarto*) or eight pages; these four leaves constitute one signature (one section of a bound book). A page measures about 6-3/4 in. × 8-1/2 in. On the other hand, a folio sheet is folded once to make two leaves or four pages; three sheets, or twelve pages, constitute a signature. The page is approximately 8-1/2 in. × 13-3/4 in.

Authorized publication occurred when a company disbanded, when money was needed but rights were to be retained, when a play failed or ran into licensing difficulties (thus, hopefully, the printed work would justify the play against the criticism), or when a play had been pirated. Authorized editions are called good quartos. Piratical publication might occur when the manuscript of a play had circulated privately, when a member of a company desired money for himself, or when a stenographer or memorizer took the play down in the theater (such a version was recognizable by inclusion of stage directions derived from an eyewitness, by garbled sections, etc.). Pirated editions are called bad quartos; there are at least five bad quartos of Shakespeare's plays.

Authenticity of Works

Usually thirty-seven plays are printed in modern collections of Shakespeare's works but some recent scholars have urged the addition of two more: *Edward III* and *Two Noble Kinsmen*. At times, six of the generally-accepted plays have been questioned: *Henry I,* Parts I, II and III, *Timon of Athens, Pericles* and *Henry VIII*. The first four are usually accepted today (one hopes all question concerning *Timon* has finally ended), but if Shakespeare did not write these plays in their entirety, he certainly wrote parts of them. Of course, collaboration in those days was common. Aside from the two long narrative poems already mentioned and the sonnets (Nos. 1-152, but not Nos. 153-154), Shakespeare's poetic output is uncertain. *The Passionate Pilgrim* (1599) contains only five authenticated poems (two sonnets and three verses from *Love's Labour's Lost*); *The Phoenix and the Turtle* (1601) may be his, but the authenticity of *A Lover's Complaint* (appended to the sonnets) is highly questionable.

Who Was Shakespeare?

At this point we might mention a problem that has plagued Shakespeare study for over a century: who was Shakespeare? Those who would like to make the author of the plays someone else — Francis Bacon or the Earl of Oxford or even Christopher Marlowe (dead long before most of the plays were written) — have used the lack of information of Shakespeare's early years and the confusion in the evidence we have been examining to advance their candidate. But the major arguments against Shakespeare show the source of these speculators' disbelief to be in classconscious snobbery and perhaps in a perverse adherence to minority opinion. The most common argument is that no one of Shakespeare's background, lack of education, and lack of aristocratic experience could know all that the author knew. But study will reveal that such information was readily available in various popular sources, that some of it lies in the literary sources used for the play, and that Shakespeare was probably not totally lacking in education or in social decorum. The more significant question of style and tone is not dealt with — nor could it successfully be raised. Bacon, for example, no matter how much we admire his mind and his writings, exhibits a writing style diametrically opposite to Shakespeare's, a style most unpoetic and often flat. The student would be wise not to waste time rehashing these unfounded theories. No such question was raised in the seventeenth or eighteenth centuries, and no serious student of the plays today doubts that Shakespeare *was* Shakespeare.

Shakespeare's Plays

Exact dates for Shakespeare's plays remain a source of debate among scholars. The following serve only as a general frame of reference.

	COMEDIES	TRAGEDIES	HISTORIES
1591			Henry VI, Part I
1592	Comedy of Errors		Henry VI, Part II
1592	Two Gentlemen of Verona		Henry VI, Part III
1593	Love's Labour's Lost	Titus Andronicus	Richard III
1594			King John
1595	Midsummer Night's Dream	Romeo and Juliet	Richard II
1596	Merchant of Venice		
1596	Taming of the Shrew		
1597			Henry IV, Part I
1598	Much Ado About Nothing		Henry IV, Part II
1599	As You Like It	Julius Caesar	
1599	Merry Wives of Windsor		Henry V
1601	Twelfth Night	Hamlet	
1602	Troilus and Cressida		
1602	All's Well That Ends Well		
1604	Measure for Measure	Othello	
1605		King Lear	
1606		Macbeth	
1607		Timon of Athens	
1607		Antony and Cleopatra	
1608	Pericles		
1609		Coriolanus	
1610	Cymbeline		
1611	Winter's Tale		
1611	Tempest		
1613			Henry VIII

Shakespeare's England

The world of Elizabethan and Jacobean England was a world of growth and change. The great increase in the middle class, and in the population as a whole, demanded a new economy and means of livelihood, a new instrument of government (one recognizing "rights" and changed class structure), a new social code and a broad base of entertainment. The invention of printing a century before had contributed to that broader base, but it was the theater that supplied the more immediate needs of the greatest numbers. The theater grew and along with it came less-educated, more money-conscious writers, who gave the people what they wanted: entertainment. But Shakespeare, having passed through a brief period of hack writing, proceeded to set down important ideas in memorable language throughout most of his career. His plays, particularly the later ones, have been analyzed by recent critics in terms of literary quality through their metaphor, verse-line, relationships with psychology and myth, and elaborate structure. Yet Shakespeare was a man of the stage, and the plays were written to be performed. Only this will fully account for the humor of a deadly serious play like *Hamlet* or the spectacle of a *Coriolanus*.

Life in London

During Shakespeare's early years there, London was a walled city of about 200,000, with seven gates providing access to the city from the east, north and west. It was geographically small and crisscrossed by narrow little streets and lanes. The various wards each had a parish church that dominated the life of the close-knit community. To the south and outside were slums and the haunts of criminal types, and farther out were the agricultural lands and huge estates. As the population increased and the central area declined, the fashionable people of the city moved toward the west, where the palace of Westminster lay. Houses were generally rented out floor by floor and sometimes room by room. Slums were common within the city, too, though close to pleasant enough streets and squares. "Merrie Olde England" was not really clean, nor were its people, for in those days that were no sewers or drains except the gutter in the middle of the street, into which garbage would be emptied to be floated off by the rain. Plague was particularly ravaging in 1592, 1593-94 (when the theaters were closed to avoid contamination) and 1603. Medical knowledge, of course, was slight; ills were "cured" by amputation, leeching and blood-letting. The city was (and still is) dominated by St. Paul's Cathedral, around which booksellers clustered on Paternoster Row.

Religious Atmosphere

Of great significance for the times was religion. Under Elizabeth, a state church had developed; it was Protestant in nature and was called Anglican (or today, Episcopalian). It had arisen from Henry VIII's break with the Pope and from a compromise with the Roman Catholics who had gained power under Mary Tudor.

The Church of England was headed by the Archbishop of Canterbury, who was to be an increasingly important figure in the early part of the seventeenth century. There were also many schismatic groups, which generally desired further departures from Roman Catholicism. Calvinists were perhaps the most numerous and important of the Protestant groups. The Puritans, who were Calvinist, wanted to "purify" the church of ritual and certain ideas, but during the 1590s they were labeled as extremists in dress and conduct.

Political Milieu

During Shakespeare's lifetime there were two monarchs: Elizabeth, 1558-1603, and James I, 1603-1625. Elizabeth was the daughter of Henry VIII and Anne Boleyn, his second wife, who was executed in 1536. After Henry's death, his son by his third wife, Jane Seymour (who died in 1537), reigned as Edward VI. He was followed by Mary Tudor, daughter of Henry's first wife, Catherine of Aragon. Mary was a Roman Catholic, who tried to put down religious dissension by persecution of both Protestants and Catholics. Nor did her marriage to Philip II of Spain endear her to the people.

Elizabeth's reign was troubled by many offers of marriage, particularly from Spanish and French nobles — all Roman Catholic — and by the people's concern for an heir to the throne. English suitors generally cancelled one another out by intrigue or aggressiveness. One of the most prominent was the Earl of Essex, Robert Devereux, who fell in and out of favor; he apparently attempted to take over the reins of control, only to be captured, imprisoned and executed in February, 1601. One claimant to the throne was Mary of Scotland, a Roman Catholic and widow of Francis II of France. She was the second cousin of Elizabeth, tracing her claim through her grandmother, who was Henry VIII's sister. Finally, settlement came with Elizabeth's acceptance of Mary's son as heir apparent, though Mary was to be captured, tried and executed for treason in 1587. Mary had abdicated the throne of Scotland in 1567 in favor of her son, James VI. His ascent to the throne of England in 1603 as James I joined the two kingdoms for the first time, although Scotland during the seventeenth century often acted independently of England.

Contemporary Events

Political and religious problems were intermingled in the celebrated Gunpowder Plot. Angry over fines that were levied upon those not attending Church of England services — primarily Roman Catholics — and offended by difficulties over papal envoys, a group of Catholics plotted to blow up Parliament, and James with it, at its first session on November 5, 1605. A cache of gunpowder was stored in the cellar, guarded by various conspirators, among them Guy Fawkes. The plot was discovered before it could be carried out and Fawkes, on duty at the time, was arrested. The execution of the plotters and the triumph of the anti-Papists led in succeeding years to celebrations in the streets and the hanging of Fawkes in effigy.

Among the most noteworthy public events during these times were the wars with the Spanish, which included the defeat of the Spanish Armada in 1588, the battle in the Lowlands in 1590-1594, the expedition to Cadiz under Essex in 1596 and the expedition to the Azores (the Islands Expedition), also under Essex, in 1597. With trading companies specially set up for colonization and exploitation, travel excited the imagination of the people: here was a new way of life, here were new customs brought back by the sailors and merchants, here was a new world to explore.

In all, the years from around 1590 to 1601 were trying ones for English people, relieved only by the news from abroad, the new affluence and the hope for the future under James. Writers of this period frequently reflect, however, the disillusionment and sadness of those difficult times.

The Elizabethan Theater

Appearance

The Elizabethan playhouse developed from the medieval inn with its rooms grouped around a courtyard into which a stage was built. This pattern was used in The Theatre, built by James Burbage in 1576: a square frame building (later round or octagonal) with a square yard, three tiers of galleries, each jutting out over the one below, and a stage extending into the middle of the yard, where people stood or sat on improvised seats. There was no cover over the yard or stage and lighting was therefore natural. Performances were held in the afternoon.

Other theaters were constructed over the years: The Curtain in 1577, The Rose in 1587 (on Bankside), The Swan in 1595 (also Bankside) and Shakespeare's playhouse, The Globe, in 1599 (not far from The Rose). There is still some question about the exact dimensions of this house, but it seems to have been octagonal, each side measuring about 36 feet, with an over-all diameter of 84 feet. It was about 33 feet to the eaves, and the yard was 56 feet in diameter. Three sides were used for backstage and to serve the needs of the players. The stage jutted out into the audience and there was no curtain. The spectators often became part of the action. Obviously, the actors' asides and soliloquies were effective under these conditions.

There was no real scenery and there were only a few major props. Thus the lines of the play had to reveal locations and movement, changes in time or place, etc. In this way, too, it was easier to establish a nonrealistic setting, for all settings were created in words. On either side of the stage were doors, within the flooring were trapdoors (for entrances of ghosts, etc.), and behind the main stage was the inner stage or recess. Here, indoor scenes (such as a court or a bedchamber) were played, and some props could be used because the inner stage was usually concealed by a curtain when not in use. It might also have served to hide someone behind the ever-present arras (hanging tapestry), like Polonius in *Hamlet*. The "chamber" was on the second level, with windows and a balcony. On the third level was another chamber, primarily for musicians.

Actors

An acting company such as the Lord Chamberlain's Men was a fellowship of ten to fifteen sharers with some ten to twelve extras,

9

three or four boys (often to play women's roles) who might become full sharers, and stagehands. There were rival companies, each with its leading dramatist and leading tragic actor and clown. The Lord Admiral's Men, organized in 1594, boasted Ben Jonson and the tragedian Edward Alleyn. Some of the rivalry of this War of the Theaters is reflected in the speeches of Hamlet, who comments on the ascendancy and unwarranted popularity of the children's companies (like the Children of Blackfriars) in the late 1590s.

The company dramatist, of course, had to think in terms of the members of his company as he wrote his play. He had to make use of the physical features and peculiar talents of the actors, making sure, besides, that there was a role for each member. The fact that women's parts were taken by boys imposed obvious limitations on the range of action. Accordingly, we often find women characters impersonating men. For example, Robert Goffe played Portia in *The Merchant of Venice*, and Portia impersonates a male lawyer in the important trial scene. Goffe also played Juliet, and Anne in *Richard III*, and Oberon in *A Midsummer Night's Dream*. The influence of an actor on the playwright can be seen, on the one hand, by noting the "humor" characters portrayed so competently by Thomas Pope, who was a choleric Mercutio in *Romeo*, a melancholic Jaques in *As You Like It*, and a sanguinary Falstaff in *Henry IV*, Part I; and by comparing, on the other hand, the clown Bottom in *A Midsummer Night's Dream*, played in a frolicsome manner by William Kempe, with the clown Feste in *Twelfth Night*, sung and danced by Robert Armin. Obviously, too, if a certain kind of character was not available within the company, then that kind of character could not be written into the play. The approach was decidedly different from ours today, where the play almost always comes first and the casting of roles second. The plays were performed in a repertory system, with a different play each afternoon. The average life of a play was about ten performances.

History of the Drama

English drama goes back to native forms developed from playlets presented at Church holidays. Mystery plays dealt with biblical stories such as the Nativity or the Passion, and miracle plays usually depicted the lives of saints. The merchant and craft guilds that came to own and produce the cycles of plays were the forerunners of the theatrical companies of Shakespeare's time. The kind of production these cycles received, either as moving pageants in the streets or as staged shows in a churchyard, influenced the late sixteenth-century production of a secular play: there was an intimacy with the audience and there was a great reliance on words rather than setting and props. Similar involvement with the stage action is experienced by audiences of the arena theater of today.

The morality play, the next form to develop, was an allegory of the spiritual conflict between good and evil in the soul of man. The *dramatis personae* were abstract virtues and vices, with at least one man representing Mankind (or Everyman, as the most popular of these plays was titled). Some modern critics see *Othello* as a kind of morality play in which the soul of Othello is vied for by the aggressively evil Iago (as a kind of Satanic figure) and passively good Desdemona (as a personification of Christian faith in all men). The Tudor interlude — a short, witty, visual play — may have influenced the subplot of the Elizabethan play with its low-life and jesting and visual tricks. In mid-sixteenth century appeared the earliest known English comedies, Nicholas Udall's *Ralph Roister Doister* and *Gammer Gurton's Needle* (of uncertain authorship). Both show the influence of the Roman comic playwright Plautus. Shakespeare's *Comedy of Errors*, performed in the 1590's, was an adaptation of Plautus' *Menaechmi*, both plays featuring twins and an involved story of confused identities. The influence of the Roman tragedian Seneca can be traced from Thomas Norton and Thomas Sackville in *Gorboduc* to *Hamlet*. Senecan tragedy is a tragedy of revenge, characterized by many deaths, much blood-letting, ghosts, feigned madness and the motif of a death for a death.

Shakespeare's Artistry

Plots

Generally, a Shakespearean play has two plots: a main plot and a subplot. The subplot reflects the main plot and is often concerned with inferior characters. Two contrasting examples will suffice: Lear and his daughters furnish the characters for the main plot of filial love and ingratitude. Gloucester and his sons enact the same theme in the subplot. Lear and Gloucester both learn that outward signs of love may be false. In *A Midsummer Night's Dream*, the town workmen (Quince, Bottom *et al.*) put on a tragic play in such a hilarious way that it turns the subject of the play — love so strong that the hero will kill himself if his loved one dies first — into farce, but this in the main plot is the "serious" plight of the four mixed-up lovers. In both examples Shakespeare has reinforced his points by subplots dealing with the same subject as the main plot.

Sources

The plots of the Elizabethan plays were usually adapted from other sources. Originality was not the sought quality; a kind of variation on a theme was. It was felt that one could better evaluate the playwright's worth by seeing what he did with a familiar tale. What he stressed, how he stressed it, how he restructured the familiar elements — these were the important matters. Shakespeare closely followed Sir Thomas North's popular translation of Plutarch's *Life of Marcus*

Antonius, for example, in writing *Antony and Cleopatra.* He modified Robert Greene's *Pandosto* and combined it with the Pygmalion myth in *The Winter's Tale,* while drawing the character of Autolycus from certain pamphlets written by Greene. The only plays for which sources have not been clearly determined are *Love's Labour's Lost* (probably based on contemporary events) and *The Tempest* (possibly based on some shipwreck account from travelers to the New World).

Verse and Prose

There is a mixture of verse and prose in the plays, partially because plays fully in verse were out of fashion. Greater variety could thus be achieved and character or atmosphere could be more precisely delineated. Elevated passages, philosophically significant ideas, speeches by men of high rank are in verse, but comic and light parts, speeches including dialect or broken English, and scenes that move more rapidly or simply give mundane information are in prose. The poetry is almost always blank verse (iambic pentameter lines without rhyme). Rhyme is used, however (particularly the couplet), to mark the close of scenes or an important action. Rhyme also serves as a cue for the entrance of another actor or some off-stage business, to point to a change of mood or thought, as a forceful opening after a passage of prose, to convey excitement or passion or sentimentality and to distinguish characters.

Shakespeare's plays may be divided into three general categories, though some plays are not readily classified and further subdivisions may be suggested within a category.

The History Play

The history play, or chronicle, may tend to tragedy, like *Richard II,* or to comedy, like *Henry IV,* Part I. It is a chronicle of some royal personage, often altered for dramatic purposes, even to the point of falsifying the facts. Its popularity may have resulted from the rising of nationalism of the English, nurtured by their successes against the Spanish, their developing trade and colonization, and their rising prestige as a world power. The chronicle was considered a political guide, like the popular *Mirror for Magistrates,* a collection of writings showing what happens when an important leader falls through some error in his ways, his thinking or his personality. Thus the history play counsells the right path by negative, if not positive, means. Accordingly, it is difficult to call *Richard II* a tragedy, since Richard was wrong and his wrongness harmed his people. The political philosophy of Shakespeare's day seemed to favor the view that all usurpation was bad and should be corrected, but not by further usurpation. When that original usurpation had been established, through an heir's ascension to the throne, it was to be accepted. Then any rebellion against the "true" king would be a rebellion against God.

Tragedy

Tragedy, in simple terms, means that the protagonist dies. Certain concepts drawn from Aristotle's *Poetics* require a tragic hero of high standing, who must oppose some conflicting force, either external or internal. The tragic hero should be dominated by a *hamartia* (a so-called tragic flaw, but really an *excess* of some character trait, e.g., pride, or *hubris*), and it is this *hamartia* that leads to his downfall and, because of his status, to the downfall of others. The action presented in the tragedy must be recognizable to the audience as real. Through seeing it enacted, the audience has its passion (emotions) raised, and the conclusion of the action thus brings release from that passion (*catharsis*). A more meaningful way of looking at tragedy in the Elizabethan theater, however, is to see it as that which occurs when essential good (like Hamlet) is wasted (through disaster or death) in the process of driving out evil (such as Claudius represents).

Comedy

Comedy in simple terms means that the play ends happily for the protagonists. Sometimes the comedy depends on exaggerations of man's eccentricities — comedy of humors; sometimes the comedy is romantic and far-fetched. The romantic comedy was usually based on a mix-up in events or confused identity of characters, particularly by disguise. It moves towards tragedy in that an important person might die and the mix-up might never be unraveled; but in the nick of time something happens or someone appears (sometimes illogically or unexpectedly) and saves the day. It reflects the structure of myth by moving from happiness to despair to resurrection. *The Winter's Tale* is a perfect example of this, for the happiness of the first part is banished with Hermione's exile and Perdita's abandonment. Tragedy is near when the lost baby, Perdita, cannot be found and Hermione is presumed dead. But Perdita reappears, as does Hermione, a statue that suddenly comes to life. Lost identities are established and confusions disappear but the mythic-comic nature of the play is seen in the reuniting of the mother, Hermione, a kind of Ceres, with her daughter, Perdita, a kind of Proserpina. Spring returns, summer will bring the harvest, and the winter of the tale is left behind — for a little while.

What is it, then, that makes Shakespeare's art so great? Perhaps we see in it a whole spectrum of humanity, treated impersonally, but with kindness and understanding. We seldom meet in Shakespeare a weeping philosopher: he may criticize, but he criticizes both sides. After he has done so, he gives the impression of saying, Well, that's the way life is; people will always be like that — don't get upset about it. This is probably the key to the Duke's behavior in *Measure for Measure* — a most unbitter comedy despite former labels. Only in *Hamlet* does Shakespeare not seem to fit this statement; it is the one play that Shakespeare, the person, enters.

As we grow older and our range of experience widens, so, too, does Shakespeare's range seem to expand. Perhaps this lies in the ambiguities of his own materials, which allow for numerous individual readings. We meet our own experiences — and they are ours alone, we think — expressed in phrases that we thought our own or our own discovery. What makes Shakespeare's art so great, then, is his ability to say so much to so many people in such memorable language: he is himself "the show and gaze o' the time."

THE TEMPEST
The Sources of the Plot

Many works are named from which Shakespeare probably took incidents, or borrowed ideas for parts of the play of *The Tempest,* but there is no known work to which the plot of the play can be positively traced.

It is quite possible, however, that Shakespeare did borrow his plot from some story which is now lost, though it may have been at one time in existence in print. We know that in the case of other plays he almost invariably founded the plot upon some well known tale, and it is consequently not an unlikely supposition that the plot of *The Tempest* had a similar origin.

AURELIO AND ISABELLA

This presumption is perhaps borne out by the fact that the poet Collins informed the laureate Thomas Warton that he had read the romance from which the play was formed, and though he named a story *Aurelio and Isabella* which, on examination, was found to contain no suggestion of such a plot, yet, as Warton says: "A useful conclusion may be drawn from it, that Shakespeare's story is somewhere to be found in an Italian novel, at least that the story preceded Shakespeare."

THE BEAUTIFUL SIDEA

There is in existence a German play, *Die Schöne Sidea* (The Beautiful Sidea) by Jacob Ayrer, a notary of Nuremberg, the plot of which resembles that of *The Tempest* so closely that critics have suggested that the two plays were in some way connected with each other. It is impossible that Ayrer's plot was taken from *The Tempest,* however, since he died in 1605, some 7 years prior to the first performance of *The Tempest* at the court of James I, in 1612.

English players had been to Nuremberg in 1604, and from them Shakespeare may have borrowed some ideas; or both plays may well have a common origin which may even yet be discovered, as well as some unknown chronicle of the union of the houses of Naples and Milan.

SOURCES FOR DIFFERENT PARTS OF THE PLAY

Many different works are named as having furnished Shakespeare with incidents or ideas for his play. Here is a list of the more important:–

1.   A pamphlet which appeared in 1601, *A Discovery of the Bermudas, otherwise called the Ile of Divels,* by Silvester Jourdan, contains the following passage:–

For the Ilandes of the Barmudas, as every man knoweth that hath heard or read of them, were never inhabited by any Christian or Heathen people, but ever esteemed and reputed a most prodigious and inchanted place, affording nothing but gusts, stormes and foule weather; which made every Navigator and Mariner to avoide them . . . Yet did we finde there the ayre so temperate

15

and the Country so abundantly fruitful of all fit necessaries for the sustentation and preservation of mans life . . . that we were there for the space of nine moneths . . . well refreshed.

This is one of several accounts of the adventures of an expedition of colonists from London to Virginia. The flagship, carrying the Admiral, Sir George Somers, was separated from the other seven ships by a storm. It was leaking badly when the Admiral spied land, and, though the Bermudas had an evil reputation, it was a case of "any port in a storm." A high tide lodged the ship between two rocks, and all escaped to the shore, where they found the climate pleasant and the land fruitful. Nine months later they had built two vessels and continued their way to Virginia. Later some of the seamen arrived in London and aroused great public interest by their story.

2. Another pamphlet was issued in 1610 in connection with the same voyage of Sir Geo. Somers, with the title *The True Declaration of the Council of Virginia,* which may also have furnished hints.

3. Florio's translation of Montaigne's Essays was published in the year 1603, and it is known that Shakespeare had a copy of the book, for there is one with the poet's autograph in the British Museum. The 30th chapter of the 1st book of the Essays contains a description of an imaginary nation of cannibals from which the following extract is taken:–

"It is a nation, would I answer Plato, that hath no kind of traffic, no knowledge of letters, no intelligence of numbers, no name of magistrate, nor of political superiority; no use of service, of riches, or of poverty; no contracts, no successions, no dividences; no occupation, but idle; no respect of kindred, but common; no apparel, but natural; no manuring of lands; no use of wine, corn, or metal."

Comparing this with Gonzalo's description of his imaginary commonwealth in Act II, Sc. 1, there is little doubt that the dramatist was familiar with the work of the Essayist, and could have borrowed ideas from him.

4. Prospero's speech in Act IV contains a number of lines that bear a certain resemblance to passages from the Earl of Sterline's tragedy of *Darius,* published at Edinburgh in 1603.

5. Hakluyt's *Voyages* (1598) may have provided some features, again there are a number of similarities in the lines of *The Tempest* and Hakluyt's *Voyages.*

6. Eden's *History of Travale in the East and West Indies,* probably supplied the name of Setebos, and likely the names Alonso, Ferdinand, Sebastian, Gonzalo and Antonio as well.

7. Raleigh's *Discovery of the large, rich, and bewtiful Empire of Guiana* (1596) in which the author speaks of "a nation of people whose heads appear not above their shoulders . . . their mouths in the middle of their breasts." With this description compare Act III, Sc. 3, 43-7:–

> *"When we were boys,*
> *Who would believe that there were mountaineers*
> *Dew-lapp'd like bulls, whose throats had hanging at 'em*
> *Wallets of flesh? or that there were such men*
> *Whose heads stood in their breasts?"*

8. Golding's *Translation of Ovid* was familiar to Shakespeare, who appears to have been indebted to it for much of Prospero's speech.

> *'Ye elves of hills, brooks, standing lakes and groves,'* etc.
> (Act V, Sc. 1, 33-50)

9. For the magical portions of the book Shakespeare may have taken suggestions from King James *Demonology* (1603); from Scot's *Discoverie of Witchcraft* and *Discours of Divels and Spirits* (1584) and from Dr. Dee, a famous magician whose library of four thousand books and seven thousand manuscripts was seized in 1583.

10. From the chapter in Philemon Holland's translation of Pliny (1601), which treats "of strange and wondrous shapes of sundrie nations," Shakespeare may have gathered general ideas of a monster in human shape, like Caliban.

Structure of the Play

GENERAL   All of the Shakespeare plays are constructed in five acts similarly developed: Act I, Introduction; Act II, Development; Act III, Crisis or Turning Point; Act IV, Complications; Act V Denouement. This works out in *The Tempest* as follows.

ACT I, INTRODUCTION   The time, place, and magic nature of the play are indicated. All the chief characters are introduced, the mariners and courtiers in Scene 1, and Prospero, Miranda, Ariel, Ferdinand, and Caliban in Scene 2. The use of magic is introduced and illustrated in the two scenes, and in the second we are given all the information required as to the past history of Prospero, Miranda, Ariel, and Caliban, and we are prepared for the love story of the play.

ACT II, DEVELOPMENT   The two scenes of Act II are parallel in development. Two groups of the shipwrecked passengers appear, courtiers in the first scene, and commoners in the second, each unknown to the other. Ariel unites himself with the former and Caliban with the latter. The first scene develops a plot to seize the throne of Naples, and in the second Stephano plans to make himself king of the island.

ACT III, CRISIS   In Scene I Ferdinand and Miranda pledge mutual love. In the second Caliban and Stephano plot the murder of Prospero. In the third, Antonio and Sebastian renew their plot against Alonso. Prospero becomes

17

aware of both plots and announces his power over the conspirators and his intention to defeat their purposes, which forms the crisis or turning point of the play.

ACT IV   Instead of the usual complications of Act IV in Shakespeare plays, this Act is rather an interlude of an antimasque to entertain the audience as well as Ferdinand and Miranda while Prospero's preparations for rewards and punishment are being completed.

ACT V, DENOUEMENT   The unfolding of all difficulties, in which all former actors are brought together before the curtain drops, appears in this Act. The marriage of Ferdinand and Miranda is blessed by Alonso, the guilty Antonio and Sebastian are punished, Alonso and Gonzalo rewarded, the rioters dismissed with physical discomfort, and Caliban restored to his former possession of the island, and Ariel is set free.

Duration of Action

The ancient Greek laws of drama, the three unities, were the Laws of Time, Place, and Action. The first required that the three or four hours needed in producing the play on the stage should represent a corresponding length of time in actual action. In the second all the events must happen in the one place. In the third, nothing must be introduced to take attention away from the subject presented, such as secondary stories. Other playwrights of Shakespeare's day clung to the Greek laws and criticized Shakespeare as an innovator unable to observe them. This later play written by him proves that he can observe the unities and at the same time preserve his freedom. The events in *The Tempest* occupy less than four hours, the action is confined to a small island, and no extraneous matter is introduced. The supernatural antimasques are not considered as part of the action.

At the beginning of the action, in Act I, Sc. 2, Prospero informs us that it is after two o'clock, "at least two glasses," and that his work must be finished by six. In Act III, Sc. 1, Miranda bids Ferdinand farewell for half an hour, and in the same scene Prospero remarks that he must carry out his business before supper time. In the next scene Caliban states that Prospero will be asleep within half an hour. Then at the close of Act V, Ariel announces that it is going on for six o'clock, and shortly afterwards, in line 136, Alonso says that it is only three hours since he was wrecked on the shore, and again in 186 he tells Ferdinand that his acquaintance with Miranda was less than three hours old. In line 223 the Boatswain says that it is only three hours since they thought their boat split. These frequent repetitions indicate that the author wished to prove to his audience that he has observed the Law of Time.

Points of Interest

Spectacular

Chief interest in the play is probably the series of unusual occurrences that challenge attention one after the other. Naming some of them, we have the play of wind and fire in the shipwreck, the foiled attempt of Ferdinand to fight a duel, the gestures, behaviour, and jests of the courtiers, the thwarted murder of Alonso, Ferdinand, Miranda, and the wood pile, the bottle of liquor and the drunkards, appearance and disappearance of the banquet, the harpy, goddesses, nymphs, and reapers, the line of garments, and the arrival one after the other of the groups of characters towards the close. Dress plays a large part in variety, rich and elaborate with the court, chaste and white of spirits, dishevelled of the drunkards and grotesque with Caliban.

Supernatural

The structure and action of the play depend almost on the use of the supernatural. It includes spirits of air, earth, fire, and water. A distinction is made between the evil of witchcraft and the good of magic at its best. Strange sounds of the island dominate the play, thunder and roaring at the wreck, thunder and lightning accompanying evil, and soft, solemn, or sweet music attending the good. The courtiers are put to sleep and awakened with songs. The banquet, goddesses, spirits, reapers, dogs, and garments appear from nowhere and mysteriously vanish. The mystery of the unknown pervades in nearly every scene.

Humour

Humour may be found in situations, speech, gestures, and actions. The humour of this play lies almost altogether in the actions, speech, and gestures of the quarreling courtiers and drunken rascals. The court jester, who normally should supply wit and humour, is too drunk and quarrelsome to exercise his inventive skill. Incidents such as the dogs chasing the rascals and the quarrel of Trinculo and Caliban depend for their humour on the skill of the performers of the play on the stage.

Romance

The world of the play lies in the imagination, a condition in which good finally prevails and evil is suitably punished or abolished. The love story is that of a courteous, correct young man, so naive at the outset that he reveals his experiences in love to a maiden who has never seen a young man before, and their love at first sight reaches maturity at once. The strange sounds of the island, the genial atmosphere and vegetation, the mysterious spirits appearing at every happening, and the control of all by Ariel create a romantic surrounding.

19

Contrasts

The use of contrast tends to bring out personality and heighten interest by placing opposites side by side. It occurs in scenes, characters, dress, and action. The terror of the storm and wreck is set off by the quiet conversation of Prospero and Miranda. The mourning of Alonso is followed by the drunken scene of Stephano and Caliban. Caliban, the earthy creature is at the other extreme of the airy Ariel. Gonzalo stands out in strong relief from Sebastian and Antonio, and Ferdinand with his court experience comes face to face with Miranda's ingenuousness. The reapers in their work-a-day dress are ridiculous in their dancing with nymphs in gossamer robes. Contrasting pairs are found in Prospero and his brother coupled with Alonso and his brother; the plot of Sebastian and Antonio is reflected in that of Stephano and Caliban.

Suspense

We find little use of this device to hold the interest of the audience because of the shortness of time and rapidity of action. Prospero tells us in advance of his intentions regarding his daughter and Ferdinand. The audience knows that Ariel will forestall the plots of the conspirators. There is a certain amount of suspense in the effect of the betrothal upon Alonso and the punishment and rewards to be meted out to those concerned.

Dramatic Situations

These are occasions when the attention of the audience becomes tense in expectation. They are allied with suspense, but the latter continues until the solution is reached, while the former is momentary. We find it in sharp exchange of sallies between Gonzalo and the Boatswain, in the threatened duel between Ferdinand and Prospero, in the drawn swords of Antonio and Sebastian, in the disappearance of the banquet just as the courtiers are moving towards it, in Prospero's listening unseen at the meeting of the lovers, and in the introduction of Miranda to Alonso.

Dramatic Irony

This situation occurs when the audience know of conditions unknown to the characters on the stage, or when some of the characters know and the others do not. This irony is used much more frequently in tragedies and historical plays than in comedies and masques. In *The Tempest* it runs quietly through the play in our knowing of the work of Ariel while the players do not. Specific examples of its occurrence are found in Prospero's listening in at the lovers, in the courtiers when in the magic circle as Prospero exposes their characters, and in Ariel's interference in the plots against Alonso and Prospero.

Fate

Fate is the intervention of some force over which human beings have no control. It is called Providence and Destiny in the play, but is by no means a characteristic of the play. But it was fate that directed Prospero's "rotten butt'' to the island, that brought Antonio and the Neapolitan court together in a ship near the island. Again, it separated the passengers from the crew after the wreck and then brought them in separate groups to land, each believing the others lost.

Nemesis

This is the Greek goddess of retributive justice, ''an eye for an eye'' who inflicts suitable punishment for the sinner. Caliban's beastliness is punished by animal pains; Antonio loses the power he usurped; the drunken state of the villains leads them into thorns and filth; and Trinculo's quarrelsome nature earns him a beating. Good deeds also bring rewards. Gonzalo's loyalty, Prospero's serious studies, and Alonso's repentance result in their final happiness.

Quotations

Very few lines of the play have become popular quotations. The best known one is found in Prospero's speech to Ferdinand after the dance of the reapers in Act IV, ''We are such stuff as dreams are made on, and our little life is rounded with a sleep''. Ariel's last song, ''Where the bee sucks, there suck I'', is another well-known line.

Philosophies

There are only two philosophers in the play, Prospero and Gonzalo. Prospero believes that life is a brief interval between the sleep of the unknown past and that of the future, that life is good, that its chief enjoyment is found in books and study, that good will finally overcome evil, and that sin must be punished. Gonzalo believes in loyalty and optimism, in making the best of a bad situation, and in the enjoyment of life, ''an acre of barren ground is better than a thousand furlongs of sea.''

Plot Summary

When Alonso, King of Naples, was returning from the wedding of his daughter to a foreign prince, his ship was overtaken by a terrible storm. In his company were Duke Antonio of Milan and other gentlemen of the court. As the gale rose in fury, and it seemed certain the vessel would split and sink, the noble travellers were forced to abandon ship and trust to fortune in the open sea.

The tempest was no chance disturbance of wind and wave. It had been raised by a wise magician, Prospero, as the ship sailed close to an enchanted island on which he and his lovely daughter Miranda were the only human inhabitants. Theirs had been a sad and curious history. Prospero was rightful Duke of Milan. Being devoted more to the study of philosophy and magic than to affairs of state, he had given much power to ambitious Antonio, his brother, who twelve years before had seized the dukedom with the aid of the crafty Neapolitan king. The conspirators set Prospero and his small daughter adrift in a boat, and they would have perished miserably had not Gonzalo, an honest counsellor, secretly stocked the frail craft with food, clothing, and the books Prospero valued most.

The helpless exiles drifted at last to an island which had been the refuge of Sycorax, an evil sorceress. There Prospero found Caliban, her son, a strange, mis-shapen creature of brute intelligence, able only to hew wood and draw water. Also obedient to Prospero's will were many good spirits of air and water, whom he had freed from torments to which the sorceress Sycorax had condemned them earlier. Ariel, a lively sprite, was chief of these.

Prospero, having used his magic arts to draw the ship bearing King Alonso and Duke Antonio close to his enchanted island, ordered Ariel to bring the whole party safely ashore, singly or in scattered groups. Ferdinand, King Alonso's son, was moved by Ariel's singing to follow the sprite to Prospero's rocky cell. Miranda, who remembered seeing no human face but her father's bearded one, at first sight fell deeply in love with the handsome young prince, and he with her. Prospero was pleased to see the young people so attracted to each other, but he concealed his pleasure, spoke harshly to them, and to test Ferdinand's mettle commanded him to perform menial tasks.

Meanwhile Alonso, Sebastian, Antonio, and Gonzalo wandered sadly along the beach, the king in despair because he believed his son drowned. Ariel, invisible in air, played solemn music, lulling to sleep all except Sebastian and Antonio. Drawing apart, they planned to kill the king and his counsellors and make Sebastian tyrant of Naples. Watchful Ariel awakened the sleepers before the plotters could act.

On another part of the island Caliban, carrying a load of wood, met Trinculo, the king's jester, and Stephano, the royal butler, both drunk. In rude sport they offered drink to Caliban. Tipsy, the loutish monster declared he would be their slave forever.

Like master, like servant. Just as Sebastian and Antonio had plotted to murder Alonso, so Caliban, Trinculo, and Stephano schemed to kill Prospero and become rulers of the island. Stephano was to be king, Miranda his consort; Trinculo and Caliban would be viceroys. Unseen, Ariel listened to their evil designs and reported the plan to Prospero.

Meanwhile Miranda had disobeyed her father to interrupt Ferdinand's task of rolling logs, and the hidden magician's commands forgotten, the two exchanged lovers' vows. Satisfied by the prince's declarations of devotion and constancy, Prospero left them to their own happy company. He, with Ariel, went to mock Alonso and his followers by showing them a banquet which vanished before the hungry castaways could taste the rich dishes. Then Ariel, disguised as a harpy, reproached them for their conspiracy against Prospero. Convinced that Ferdinand's death was punishment for his own crime, Alonso was moved to repentance for his cruel deed.

Returning to his cave, Prospero released Ferdinand from his hard toil. While spirits dressed as Ceres, Iris, Juno, nymphs, and reapers entertained Miranda and the prince with a pastoral masque, Prospero suddenly remembered the schemes which had been devised by Caliban and the drunken servants. Told to punish the plotters, Ariel first tempted them with a display of kingly garments; then, urging on his fellow spirits in the shapes of fierce hunting dogs, he drove them howling with pain and rage through bogs and brier patches.

Convinced at last that the King of Naples and his false brother Antonio had repented the evil deed they had done him years before, Prospero commanded Ariel to bring them into the enchanted circle before the magician's cell. Ariel soon returned, luring by strange, beautiful music the king, Antonio, Sebastian, and Gonzalo. At first they were astonished to see Prospero in the appearance and dress of the wronged Duke of Milan. Prospero confirmed his identity, ordered Antonio to restore his dukedom, and severely warned Sebastian not to plot further against the king. Finally he took the repentant Alonso into the cave, where Ferdinand and Miranda sat playing chess. There was a joyful reunion between father and son at this unexpected meeting, and the king was completely captivated by the beauty and grace of Miranda. During this scene of reconciliation and rejoicing, Ariel appeared with the master and boatswain of the wrecked ship; they reported the vessel safe and ready to continue the voyage. The three grotesque conspirators were driven in by Ariel, and Prospero released them from their spell. Caliban was ordered to prepare food and set it before the guests. Prospero invited his brother and the King of Naples and his train to spend the night in his cave.

Before he left the island, Prospero dismissed Ariel from his service, leaving that sprite free to wander as he wished. Ariel promised calm seas and auspicious winds for the voyage back to Naples and Milan, where Prospero would journey to take possession of his lost dukedom and to witness the marriage of his daughter and Prince Ferdinand.

Summaries and Commentaries
by Act and Scene

ACT I • SCENE 1

Summary

The play opens on a ship in the midst of a bad storm at sea. The ship's master curtly tells the boatswain to get the crew fighting the storm, but the latter has no sooner started giving his orders to the sailors than he is interrupted by the panicked entrance of the ship's royal passengers.

Alonso, the King of Naples, speaks to the boatswain, but he has no respect for royalty during such troubles at sea. "What cares these roarers for the name of king?" he asks the meddlesome passengers. When they ignore the boatswain's repeated order to go back to their cabins, he pays no further attention to them. Sebastian and Antonio, two of the courtiers, resort to cursing the sailors trying to save the ship. Though equally fearful of sinking, Gonzalo, an older courtier, makes light of the situation by saying that the boatswain is so rude he must be destined to be hanged. Thus, he's not likely to be drowned, and, with him aboard, the ship is safe. But this half-hearted joke doesn't calm anyone. In fact, by this time, the passengers are deserting the ship for the open waves, and Gonzalo's last words, "I would fain die a dry death," hold out little hope for their survival.

Commentary

This is a boisterous scene, which starts the play off with a dramatic spectacle. It is designed to catch the audience's attention as they wonder whether or not the ship will make it through the storm.

Today, theatrical storms can be re-created with modern staging devices, i.e., intricate lighting changes, pre-recorded sound effects, perhaps mechanical methods of jostling pieces of scenery to suggest the crashing waves, or even wind- or rain-making machines. In Shakespeare's day, of course, such options did not exist. The storm's wild noises were possibly made with cymbals and drums, and the sailor's yells by actors off-stage. But the most important way for the playwright to suggest the storm was to show its effect on the characters aboard the ship. With typical skillfulness, Shakespeare shows how the entire court party is frightened, at the same time as he begins to delineate certain characters by their various reactions to the storm.

Alonso, the king, makes a feeble attempt to command the boatswain's attention, but he fails — foreshadowing his lack of control over the events about to unfold. Sebastian, the king's brother, and Antonio, the Duke of Milan, take out their fears by cursing and taunting the sailors, showing the first sign of their cynical humour and complete lack of belief in any higher power that could preserve them through the storm. In fact, their last exchange only furthers their first impression as self-seeking individuals who think only of themselves in a crisis:

> Antonio: Let's all sink with th' King.
> Sebastian: Let's take leave of him.

Only Gonzalo, the older courtier, emerges as one trying to cling to his sense of humour, with the attempted joke about the boatswain. One of his last statements ("The wills above be done") shows that he, unlike the other two, has some faith in an ultimate authority that is ordering earthly events. The scene ends on a hopeless note, leaving the audience in suspense about the fate of the ship and its passengers.

This storm, representing as it does chaos, violence and disruption, gives the play its title.

ACT I • SCENE 2

Summary
This scene, the longest in the play, can be divided into three main parts:
1. Prospero's tale to Miranda
2. The introductions of Ariel and Caliban
3. The initial meeting of Ferdinand and Miranda

The first two provide a flashback to previous events by explaining how the play's current situation came to be, while the third provides the first contact between the young couple that will form the play's romantic interest. These three parts are summarized below.

1. Miranda tells her father she's seen a terrible storm and a shipwreck off the coast of the island. Prospero says he caused the storm, and he is protecting everyone who was on board from harm with his magical powers, so she is not to worry. Then he recounts the story of how they came to be on the island, a story which he has often started but never finished. Prospero says that 12 years ago he was the rightful Duke of Milan. But because he was more interested in studying philosophy and magic, he left most of the state's affairs to his brother Antonio to look after. Antonio organized matters to his own advantage, growing more powerful as Prospero continued to neglect what was happening around him. Eventually, Antonio made a secret pact with the King of Naples for his help to oust his brother. So one night an army gathered outside the city gates, and Antonio let them inside, where they seized Prospero and his then three-year-old daughter.

Miranda interrupts to ask why they weren't killed on the spot. Prospero replies that he was still too popular with his people to be murdered outright, so the conspirators had to do something that seemed less evil. Therefore, the two were put aboard a rotted old boat with no mast nor sails and were left to drift to their deaths. But Gonzalo, a noble of Naples who was in charge of this operation, generously provided them with food, water, clothes and Prospero's most important books on magic. Thus provided for, they survived until they drifted to an island, where Prospero has brought up his daughter ever since. The story finished, Miranda asks her father why he caused the recent storm. Prospero replies that his enemies have been brought close to him in an opportunity that he must seize. Then he magically puts her to sleep.

2. Now Prospero summons Ariel, an airy spirit in his command, who describes how he staged the storm according to his master's wishes. With great balls of fire, tremendous flashes of lightning and claps of thunder, Ariel so terrified all the passengers that they jumped into the sea. But he has brought them all safely to shore, in small groups at various places. The crew stayed with the ship, which was now in a quiet bay with the sailors below decks in a charmed sleep. The rest of the fleet, dispersed during the storm, have since regrouped and started back to Naples, thinking the king's ship has been lost.

This was a lot of work, and Ariel is not eager for more. But Prospero reminds him of how he was freed from the evil spell of the witch Sycorax, who had controlled the island before Prospero arrived. She died leaving Ariel, too delicate to do her foul bidding, trapped in a pine tree. Prospero released Ariel on the understanding that he would serve him. Prospero promises to free the spirit in two days if he performs well until then. Ariel is grateful and hurries off to do Prospero's bidding.

Now Prospero wakes up Miranda, and we meet Caliban, the half-human son of the witch Sycorax, who enters cursing them both. Caliban complains that he trusted them when they first arrived — showing them all around the island — and that they treated him well then, but they have now reduced him to a prisoner in a tiny corner of the island he once ruled. Prospero retorts that they were indeed kind to him at first, teaching him how to speak and many other things, until he tried to attack Miranda. Since then they have kept him as their slave, to carry wood and do other menial tasks.

"You taught me language, and my profit on't/ Is, I know how to curse," replies Caliban. Prospero threatens him with horrible pains unless he's obedient, and, grumbling, Caliban leaves to resume his tasks.

3. Now Ariel returns, luring Ferdinand, King Alonso's son, with sweet music. Ferdinand believes his father has died during the storm, and the words Ariel sings reinforce this impression. When Miranda and Ferdinand see each other, they fall in love at first sight, as Prospero had

planned. But he does not want his daughter to be so easily conquered, "lest too light winning/Make the prize light," so he speaks sharply to Ferdinand. He accuses him of not being heir to the throne of Naples as he claims, but a spy trying to steal the island from him. Prospero says he will put him in chains and give him sea-water to drink and dry roots to eat. When Ferdinand tries to resist, Prospero prevents him from moving with a spell. Miranda begs her father to release him, but he tells her to be quiet. Ferdinand is so taken with Miranda that he accepts his capture with these words:

> Might I but through my prison once a day
> Behold this maid. All corners else o' th' earth
> Let liberty make use of. Space enough
> Have I in such a prison.

> (Act I, Sc. 2, 490-93)

They exit, Miranda pleading with her father, and Prospero telling her not to make such a fuss over Ferdinand.

Commentary

This scene completes the first act of the play, which Shakespeare traditionally used as his introduction. By the end of Act I in a Shakespeare play, all the major characters, the setting and the central dilemmas of the play have usually been introduced to the audience. In fact, this is the case in *The Tempest*.

The basically negative characters of the courtiers were presented in Scene 1, and the more positive figures of Prospero, Miranda, Ariel, Caliban and Ferdinand in Scene 2. The ocean was the setting of the first scene, the island for the second. Flashbacks to Prospero's loss of his dukedom and arrival on the island, plus explanations of his hold over both Ariel and Caliban, have been provided. His magical skills were displayed in both scenes and explained in Scene 2. Now he is seen preparing to gain revenge on his enemies, who have been magically delivered into his hands. The way has also been made for the love story between Ferdinand and Miranda, and we have already seen Prospero take on the role of the disapproving parent who blocks this natural attraction, a situation typical of Shakespeare's romances.

The dilemmas that emerge include the chaotic sea versus the well-ordered life of the island; the deceit and treachery of the courtiers pitted against Prospero's magical abilities; and the former freedom of Ariel and Caliban contrasted with their present servitude.

Yet while all of this exposition is done in the first act according to Shakespeare's custom, the sheer volume of background information he has revealed is quite unusual for him. His concern that the audience not miss the details of Prospero's tale is revealed by Prospero's frequent reminders (supposedly to Miranda but in fact to the audience) to stay awake and pay attention. Looking a little closer, the reason for this unusual approach becomes clear. In Shakespeare's other plays, he generally begins the first act somewhere close to the start of the chain of events that form its plot. But in *The Tempest*, these events began 12 years earlier, when Prospero was ousted from Milan. In effect, this play starts near the end of its chain of events. Even if Shakespeare had shortened this intervening time span, it would have made the play quite cumbersome and impractical to actually show all these events, including the take-over of Milan, the storm, the landing of the castaways on the island, the meetings with Ariel and Caliban, etc. Therefore, he has Prospero describe all this, under the theatrical guise of telling the story to Miranda, and by having brief discussions with Ariel and Caliban when they complain about their slavery.

But many think there is another reason for Prospero's lengthy exposition. Shakespeare was often criticized in his time for not observing the classical rules of playwriting. Chief among these was what Aristotle called the preservation of the unities of Place, Time and Action. This meant that an ideal play was supposed to take place all in the same setting, within a time span of 24 hours, and deal with just a single main subject. *The Tempest* was perhaps intended as Shakespeare's final play and his farewell to the stage. (Although he seems to have collaborated on at least one other some years later.) In any case, perhaps he set out here to prove that he could preserve the unities if he wished, confining the action to a small island, stressing the passage of time throughout and ultimately wrapping it up in only four hours, and focusing the entire thrust of the action upon Prospero's righting of the wrong that was done to him — even deliberately limiting the love story and using all the comic characters to contribute to this essential centerpiece.

The sheer bulk of this scene, one of the longest Shakespeare ever wrote, shows how difficult artistic compromises can sometimes result from what seems to be a simple decision. If Shakespeare deliberately set out to write a play that preserved the classical unities, this scene (or something like it) would be bound to result: a lengthy exposition of past events that set the scene for the quick resolution of the present action.

The remainder of this commentary discusses the three main parts of this scene (as noted in the summary) in more detail.

1. The scene begins with Miranda's dramatic description of the storm and the shipwreck off the island. Miranda speaks of "the wild waters in this roar" and the fiery sky that "would pour down stinking pitch" if it weren't for the sea rising up and seeming to extinguish its fires. Here Shakespeare uses language to heighten the spectacle of the storm in an effort to dramatize with words what cannot be shown on stage.

Miranda's character is also suggested during these passages when she says, "I have suffered/With those that I saw suffer . . .," adding that she would have stopped the storm if she had any power to do so. Her naïve assumption that there must have been "some noble creature" aboard the ship when it sank further emphasizes her natural innocence and compassion for others.

But Prospero breaks in on her worries with his explanation of their own arrival on the island. He clearly feels Miranda is now mature enough to hear the whole story, perhaps signalling that she is about to begin a more independent phase of her life. Prospero's story sets up a tension between worldly and spiritual concerns that will continue throughout the play.

In a way, Prospero has been the author of his own undoing, like a typical tragic figure in Shakespeare. *The Tempest* belongs to the playwright's period of later romances, which combine elements of both tragedy and comedy, so Prospero does not fall completely into oblivion for his failure. Instead, he re-emerges to set things right, having already corrected the character flaw that was his initial downfall: his exaggerated thirst for knowledge, which made him "to my state grew stranger, being transported/And rapt in secret studies." Although this knowledge was at that time his undoing, the occult wisdom he learned then, combined with his present watchfulness over practical details, has made Prospero more than a match for his morally corrupted rivals. His anger, which stirs as he recalls Antonio's treachery, and the dramatic nature of the events themselves are factors that help to sustain the audience's interest during this re-telling. Prospero begins his tale by first removing his magician's robes, perhaps to take on the more personal role of Miranda's father, and then donning them again at the end of his tale. He also punctuates his speech with frequent commands to stay awake and pay attention. Beyond the point made above that these comments are in reality aimed at the audience, they perhaps have an ironic intent as well. Prospero's whole story is an admission of his earlier error in judgement. Here he is not only telling Miranda the story directly but is perhaps telling her in a subtle way not to repeat his mistake of growing inattentive to the immediate concerns of daily life.

When Prospero concludes by telling his daughter that now his enemies are close by, and he can right their wrongdoing, the audience is prepared for the main thrust of the play's action in the scenes that follow.

2. In this middle part of the scene, the characters of Ariel and Caliban are introduced. These two are opposites in many ways. Ariel is a spirit of the wind and represents the higher elemental forces of air and fire, as he trips lightly and invisibly across the island, playing music and spouting delicate poetry. Caliban is a beast of the woods, closer to the

lower elements of earth and water (he is even described as having webbed feet), labouring heavily around the island with his burdens and spewing foul curses at his masters. While Ariel travels freely "On the curl'd clouds," Caliban lives in "this hard rock," some kind of cave where Prospero keeps him confined until he needs him. Neither is human but for different reasons — Ariel being beyond humanity at the ethereal end of the scale, unable to feel emotions; and Caliban being beneath humanity at the animal end, unable to think rationally.

These contrasts are revealed in their language, even in the very first speeches each makes in the play. Compare Ariel's hearty, good-natured greeting to Prospero:

> All hail, great master! Grave sir, hail! I come
> To answer thy best pleasure; be't to fly,
> To swim, to dive into the fire, to ride
> On the curl'd clouds. To thy strong bidding task
> Ariel and all his quality.
>
> (Act I, Sc. 2, 189-93)

with Caliban's vengeful oaths on his first appearance:

> As wicked dew as e'er my mother brush'd
> With raven's feather from unwholesome fen
> Drop on you both! A south-west blow on ye
> And blister you all o'er!
>
> (Act I, Sc. 2, 321-24)

Yet for all their differences, the two represent something alike, two natural forces both held in check by Prospero's magical skill. Both are somewhat irritated about their restrictions — Ariel pleads for his liberty and Caliban bemoans the earlier days when he ruled the island himself.

Both characters carry the action forward throughout the play, Ariel as the chief instrument of Prospero's will, and Caliban as the instigator of a plan to oust Prospero. Ariel is involved with the primary plot, while Caliban is part of a parallel sub-plot that serves as a foil, or reflection, of the treacherous ambitions of the courtiers.

More specifically, Ariel's description of how he staged the storm and brought the ship's passengers safely ashore in several small groups, foreshadows the different purgative experiences that Prospero will put each group through in the coming acts.

And, in this scene, Caliban helps raise an idea important to the play — the notion of "natural" as opposed to "civilized" states of being. Although we would expect the offspring of a totally evil witch to be a completely brutish, malignant presence, Caliban has an occasional redeeming thought. He even describes how at first he appreciated the kindness and teachings of Prospero:

        . . . When thou camest first,
Thou strok'dst me and mad'st much of me; wouldst give me
Water with berries in't, and teach me how
To name the bigger light, and how the less,
That burn by day and night; and then I lov'd thee
                                        (Act I, Sc. 2, 332-36)

Caliban, in return, showed Prospero all the secrets of the island. But
these harmonious relations broke down after Caliban tried to rape
Miranda, and Prospero has kept him as a slave and beast of burden
ever since.

Despite his best efforts to educate Caliban, Prospero says, his
"vile race . . . had that in't which good natures/Could not abide to be
with" and he is beyond hope of redemption.

Although the idea that magic is such a powerful force that its practitioners can rule over others seems silly to us today, it had an almost
universal acceptance in more superstitious Elizabethan times. When
Prospero mentions the "foul witch Sycorax" who was banished from
Algiers for her "sorceries terrible," the audience would immediately
understand that Sycorax used "black magic," as opposed to Prospero's
powers, which are derived from "white magic." The difference is that
the first is used for selfish or materialistic ends, while the second is used
benevolently to promote proper moral ends or cast mild, beneficial
spells. While the first suggests Satanism, human sacrifice and devil-
worship, the second suggests love potions, herbal remedies and mildly
pagan blessings on homes, fields and country — a power no more
disturbing than the sight of a good luck charm.

3. In the final part of this scene, Prospero's pre-ordained love-
match between Ferdinand and Miranda begins to develop. As he enters
the scene, led by Ariel's music, Ferdinand already suspects he is being
worked on by some superhuman presence. Ariel's first song is an invitation to dance by the sea-shore, and his second is a richly poetic stanza
well worth quoting in full.

Full fathom five thy father lies;
Of his bones are coral made;
Those are pearls that were his eyes;
Nothing of him that doth fade
But doth suffer a sea-change
Into something rich and strange.
Sea nymphs hourly ring his knell:
Hark! now I hear them — Ding-dong bell
                                        (Act I, Sc. 2, 396-404)

The line "Those are pearls that were his eyes" is repeated three times in one of the most important poems of the 20th century, T.S. Eliot's *The Wasteland*. One interpretation of *The Wasteland*, a rich and complex work, is that it portrays people stunted by their own pettiness, who brood over various possible disasters (death by water is named as one), not realizing that these are actually their routes to an important reawakening. In his note at the end of the poem, Eliot acknowledges *The Tempest* as one of his sources.

Ariel's song itself is an invocation of Ferdinand's supposedly dead father. His bones have turned to coral, his eyes to pearl. Everything about him has undergone a change from the impermanent materials of living flesh to the incorruptible substances of the earth, sings Ariel. But, in this way, he has become something "rich and strange," so it is perhaps not necessary to mourn him so sadly. It will be Alonso's later repentence for scheming against Prospero — his change of character that was set into motion by the stormy seas — that redeems him after his ordeals on the island. In fact, all the redeemable passengers emerge from their stay on the island, after the apparent disaster of the tempest and the trials that follow it, as renewed and more virtuous characters. Ariel's storm has brought disruption, chaos and destruction, contrasted with Ariel's music, which brings peace, harmony and restoration.

Ariel leads Ferdinand to Miranda, and, as Prospero has planned, they rapidly fall in love. This is one of Prospero's ways to ensure his re-emergence into power, by unifying his family with that of his rival, the King of Naples. On another level, this shows the power of love conquering all and of forgiveness healing the wounds of the past. But he cannot allow the young couple to know his plan. Prospero shows his subtle grasp of psychology when he says:

> . . . But this swift business
> I must uneasy make, lest too light winning
> Makes the prize light.
>
> (Act I, Sc. 2, 450-52)

Prospero treats Ferdinand harshly to fill his role as a protective parent, but also to emphasize how much he has learned from his previous mistakes. He is no longer overly trusting. He watches carefully a treacherous associate like Antonio, an unbridled brute like Caliban, or even a prospective but untested son-in-law like Ferdinand.

He plays down the good qualities of Ferdinand to Miranda, calling him just another man that "eats, and sleeps, and hath such senses/As we have," someone who is "something stain'd/With grief," who "hath lost his fellows/And strays about to find 'em" rather like a lost sheep. Prospero can evaluate the youth realistically and challenges Miranda, who has much less experience, to do the same, to see beyond

"The fringed curtains of thine eye." But to Miranda, Ferdinand is "A thing divine" and "noble" — she has "no ambition/To see a goodlier man."

This rapid infatuation is not meant to be completely realistic, as these two young lovers are not intended to be taken as naturalistic figures going through a typical courtship. For one thing, there isn't time (if the playwright is to preserve the unity of Time) for anything else except the instant bond of love at first sight. For another, we know that this play was written to be performed at the wedding of King James' daughter Elizabeth to a German ruler — another reason for the lovers, whom the bride and groom would no doubt see as themselves, to be idealized figures of youthful purity and innocence. Had Shakespeare added the blemishes of imperfection that usually round out his characters and make them more believeable, the play's reception might not have been so positive. By this token we can see Prospero, the wise and temperate magician, as a figure that King James himself would have identified with.

ACT II • SCENE 1

Summary
Here the largest group of courtiers from the ship are seen on the island, bad-tempered after their misadventure. Gonzalo tries to cheer up Alonso, telling him they are lucky to be alive, but the king is saddened by the supposed death of his son. To relieve their discontentment, Sebastian and Antonio unleash a series of puns aimed at Gonzalo. Sebastian then says it's all the king's fault for marrying off his daughter to the king of Tunis, causing the need for this journey in the first place. Gonzalo criticizes Sebastian for his lack of sensitivity and continues his patter, aimed at distracting the king. Although Alonso is not interested, Gonzalo presses on, saying that if he were ruler of the island, he would keep it in a completely uncivilized state — with no money, commerce, learning, laws, servants, masters, farming, work, technology or weapons allowed to intrude upon its natural state. As Sebastian and Antonio begin to ridicule this vision, Ariel enters the scene, putting everyone except these two to sleep.

Antonio gives Sebastian the idea of killing his brother the king and seizing his kingdom. Thinking Ferdinand is drowned and Alonso's daughter Claribel too distant in Tunis to succeed Alonso, Sebastian realizes he could easily become the next king. He recalls that Antonio similarly overthrew his brother and asks if his conscience bothers him. "I feel not/This deity in my bosom," answers Antonio. They agree to draw their swords, one to kill Alonso and the other Gonzalo. They judge the other men to be docile enough to go along with their new rulers. But Ariel awakens Gonzalo, who rouses the others with a shout, and they all see the two standing in their midst with their weapons out. Sebastian comes up with a lame excuse about hearing a roar in the distance, which sounded like lions, that put them on their guard. Afraid of encountering these animals, the whole party heads for another part of the island to continue the search for Ferdinand.

Commentary

A large part of this scene is devoted to courtly humour, through which the differing characters of Gonzalo, Antonio and Sebastian are sketched in more detail. Elizabethan audiences were delighted by witty word-play, and the most popular playwrights were those who, like Shakespeare, could produce a running stream of puns. Although appreciated by all classes, this style of wit was practised mainly by the educated upper-classes.

Antonio and Sebastian give vent to their cynical feelings in a series of puns aimed at Gonzalo, whose persistent good humour irritates them. Gonzalo sees on the island "everything advantageous to life," adding "How lush and lusty the grass looks! how green!", and even exclaims how their garments, rather than being spoiled from the salt water, look like they've been freshly dyed. Antonio, on the other hand, says the island contains no means of support for them, calls the ground "tawny" (or dull brown), and suggests Gonzalo's clothes look like they were pulled out of the sea by a fisherman. For every positive word Gonzalo speaks, Antonio offers a negative, and Sebastian follows up with another.

This is done deliberately to characterize the three courtiers in distinct ways. Gonzalo is an honest, naturally good person, who looks on the bright side and is happy just to be alive. Although he is misguided in his persistent attempts to distract Alonso from his grief, Gonzalo is only showing concern for his fellow man. Not so is Antonio, a brooding, deceitful man, perpetually cynical and scheming, a product of the corrupting influences of court, whose only thoughts for anyone else are how he can manipulate them into helping him. He has no regard for the king, either, as a person suffering the loss of his son, or as the monarch whose power he is supposed to uphold. Sebastian is another cynic, although he lacks the initiative of Antonio and is always following his lead. He is a man without moral strength, who can be talked into killing his own brother in the space of five minutes.

The contrast between these three characters is further amplified by several developments later in the scene. For one, Sebastian peevishly complains to the king about going to Tunis in the first place and is then rebuked by Gonzalo for his impatience: "You rub the sore/When you should bring the plaster." Never one to disagree, Sebastian immediately sees Gonzalo's point and does not attempt a witty retort, although Antonio does. Even more significant is the scheme, hatched by Antonio and Sebastian while the others are in a charmed sleep, to murder Alonso and Gonzalo, and take over Naples.

Again, it is Antonio who initiates this plot by putting the notion into Sebastian's head. He suggests that since Ferdinand, the son, is drowned and Claribel, the daughter, is far away in Tunis, Sebastian is the next rightful heir to Alonso's throne. He compares death to sleep and says their intended victims would be no worse off if they were killed than they are now, asleep on the shore. When Sebastian asks whether Antonio felt any remorse after similarly overthrowing his brother, Prospero, Antonio replies that he has never found his conscience to cause him any pain. They agree to the plot, but ironically it is Gonzalo who awakes in the middle of their attempt, rousing the others and forcing them to postpone their plans.

A further example of the contrasting characters of these three is shown in their reaction to Gonzalo's description of the Utopia, or ideal state, he visualizes for the island. Gonzalo says he would ban every element of civilized society and keep the island in an unspoiled, native condition:

> Letters should not be known; riches, poverty,
> And use of service, none; contract, succession,
> Bourn, bound of land, tilth, vineyard, none;
> No use of metal, corn, or wine, or oil;
> No occupation; all men idle, all;
> And women too, but innocent and pure;
> No sovereignty. . . . Treason, felony,
> Sword, pike, knife, gun, or need of any engine
> Would I not have. . . .
>
> (Act II, Sc. 1, 145-56)

This vision has no impact on Sebastian and Antonio, the products of the completely man-made world of the court and city. Instead of considering the possibilities such a state might offer, they immediately start to pin-point its logical inconsistencies — for instance, that Gonzalo has said if he were king he'd set up a state where there were no kings. Their comments are further proof that their cleverness is always used to criticize and negate others, never to build up and reassure them.

This speech of Gonzalo's is central to understanding one level of the play. The idea of a completely unspoiled state is borrowed from a French philosopher, Michel Montaigne. He first expressed this idea in his *Essays*, a book that Shakespeare is thought to have read. In one of his essays, "Of Cannibals," Montaigne contrasts the natural life of the "savages" found in the New World with the civilized European living in the Old World. This essay makes the radical suggestion that civilization is an artificial and corrupting force, while the natural way of life of native peoples makes them much stronger and healthier — an idea which later came to be known as the theory of the "noble savage."

The idea that the natural is better than the artificial has been passed down in many different forms to our own day and survives most notably in the "back to the land" movement that began in the 1960s. The attraction of organic fruit and vegetables, the development of renewable forms of energy and the conservation of wilderness and endangered species are other contemporary expressions of this same basic sentiment. In Shakespeare's time, though, all these developments were quite unheard of, and Montaigne's views were held by only a few.

The idea that the island could actually be made as Gonzalo describes it — free of labour and money, masters and slaves, farming and fighting, and any advanced skills — is dismissed by Antonio and Sebastian. In fact, were everyone as harmless and good-natured as Gonzalo, such an idealistic vision could perhaps be realized, but it is individuals such as the other two, who prey on others for their own advancement, that make it impossible to attain.

Caliban's name may be a deliberate rearrangement, or anagram, of Montaigne's word "cannibal." He is another argument against the supremacy of the natural state and the possibility of attaining a society unspoiled by any hint of civilization.

ACT II • SCENE 2

Summary

Caliban enters, cursing Prospero for his labours, then hears Trinculo, the jester, approaching. Seeing his wild costume and fearing he is another of Prospero's spirits coming to torment him, Caliban lies down on the ground to hide. Trinculo, who swam ashore alone, enters singing a sailor's song. He spots the strange looking creature and makes a long clownish inspection of him, until he hears thunder and, thinking a downpour is about to begin, crawls under Caliban's loose garments to take shelter.

Stephano, another clownish character described as a "drunken butler," enters the scene. After drifting ashore clinging to a barrel of wine and making a portable container out of birch-bark, Stephano has been wandering about the island drinking. By now he is quite drunk. He, too, goes through an investigation of what now looks like some bizarre four-legged creature of the island — making the same point Trinculo did earlier: that he could earn a small fortune displaying such a creature in side-shows across Europe. Caliban cries out, so Stephano pours several drinks into his mouth. Then Trinculo speaks too. After a comical exchange, Stephano pulls him out from under Caliban's cloak, and they have a happy reunion, telling each other how they escaped drowning.

Caliban has by now grown tipsy from his unaccustomed drink and tells Stephano he'll show him the island, catch food for him and serve him instead of Prospero. They all exit drunkenly, Caliban singing about his new-found friends: " 'Ban, 'Ban, Ca — Caliban/ Has a new master. Get a new man."

Commentary

This scene is provided as comic relief and relies on one of the standard comic routines still being used today: the drunk. The sight of the monstrous Caliban, Trinculo in the colourful costume of the court jester, and Stephano, the self-declared king of the island, all reeling around the scene in various stages of intoxication, makes a hilarious spectacle. The earthy humour of these characters, with their sailor's song, drunkenness and mildly profane suggestions ("kiss the book" meaning "take a drink"), is juxtaposed, or deliberately contrasted with, the courtly witticisms of the previous scene. In terms of the plot, this scene shows the formation of this threesome, who will stick together until the end of the play.

The theme of natural versus civilized life is touched on several times. The idea of both Stephano and Trinculo taking Caliban to Europe to be displayed in a side-show is an obvious comment on some of the cruder forms of entertainment found within a supposedly civilized state. As well, Caliban's exalted praises of Stephano and his drink — "That's a brave god and bears celestial liquor," "Hast thou not dropp'd from heaven?" — are insightful predictions of what often happened when Europeans reached North America in the century after Shakespeare. The highest fruit of civilization offered to Caliban by the new arrivals to his shore is liquor, itself a product of man's technology (and one of the substances expressly ruled out in Gonzalo's perfect commonwealth). Both these things — the side-show and the abuse of liquor — are examples of the corrupting forces of civilization on the "noble savage" that Caliban represents.

Caliban's lyrical flights of poetry — both in cursing his tormenters and celebrating his island home — show him capable of a finer sensibility than the depraved duo of Stephano and Trinculo. If anything, his error in this scene is to tolerate their presence and accept their gift of liquor instead of keeping to himself.

While Caliban speaks in verse at both the beginning and the end of this scene, the other two speak in prose throughout. As well as providing a certain refreshing break to the ear, Shakespeare generally used prose to signify the coarser speech of the characters from lower stations in life, reserving verse for the higher characters. Caliban can be seen as falling to a lower moral plane when in contact with the two drunkards, regaining himself only when he remembers that his place is to serve, although he has substituted a new and unworthy master, Stephano, for his previous stern but proper overlord, Prospero. Even Trinculo points this out, when he says, "A most ridiculous monster, to make a wonder of a poor drunkard!"

In this way, although Caliban has regained the reassuring outer form of his true station of servitude, he has lost its essential value as a restraint on his excessive drives. Stephano has neither the moral insight nor the magical skills that Prospero uses to curb Caliban, so the audience realizes that the slave's association with this master is bound to end badly.

Shakespeare's second act has been used to develop the play's two main currents of evil — the calculated conspiracy of Antonio and Sebastian in the first scene, and the uncontrollable animal urges of Caliban and the two drunkards in the second. In addition, when the drunken Stephano declares "we will inherit here," he echoes the earlier plot of the courtiers to seize power from Alonso.

Antonio represents the treachery and intrigue that can take root in even the highest level of civilization, the royal court, while Caliban shows the unfocused desires of the savage that can afflict even the lowliest drunkard. These two sub-plots have been provided, some argue, to contradict Gonzalo's vision of a naturalistic state unhampered by any intrusion of civilization. When individuals such as Antonio and Caliban exist, it seems unlikely for Gonzalo's Utopian state to ever come into being.

ACT III • SCENE 1

Summary
Ferdinand enters, carrying the wood that Prospero has instructed him to pile up as one of his punishments for invading the island. Miranda comes by to speak with him, thinking her father is at home, but Prospero is actually hidden close by, watching the couple. Miranda asks Ferdinand to take a break or let her carry the wood for a while, but he refuses. He asks her name and declares he's never seen such a perfect woman. Miranda blurts out, "Do you love me?" and Ferdinand swears ("O heaven, O earth, bear witness to this sound") that he does. Miranda bursts into tears, saying that although she's not worthy, she'll be his wife if he wants her. He instantly agrees, and Prospero, from his hiding place, comments on how pleased he is that everything is working out as he planned.

Commentary
This quick courtship scene between Ferdinand and Miranda is not intended to be a realistic depiction of passion between two lovers, but an idealized portrayal of love between two innocents. Who can imagine someone proposing as rapidly as these two do, after spending perhaps

ten minutes' time together in their lives? Again, as in Act I Scene 2, this rapid development of the affection between Ferdinand and Miranda is the only possible way to accomplish a successful romance within the four hour time-span of the play's events. The playwright is perhaps conceding that these characters cannot be developed as realistic characters in such a short span, so he won't make any attempt to do so.

The initial entrance of Ferdinand *"bearing a log"* echoes the entrance of Caliban in Act II Scene 2 *"with a burden of wood."* Each have received a similar task, but each goes about it quite differently.

While Ferdinand's first instinct was to resist, he rapidly accepts the necessity of his toil as a way to prove his love for Miranda. Ferdinand accepts Prospero's lesson that sacrifice, discipline and hard labours are needed to win Miranda.

Yet Caliban cannot learn this lesson, and his resistance is ongoing, as is his punishment. He is guided only by instinct and therefore resents any suggestion of external control. By not accepting the necessity of submission, discipline and uncomplaining work, Caliban makes himself miserable every day.

ACT III • SCENE 2

Summary

Caliban, Stephano and Trinculo are, by this time, quite drunk. Trinculo taunts Caliban and is warned by Stephano to "keep a good tongue in your head." Then Caliban describes his plan to murder Prospero while he's asleep so they can take over the island. Ariel, invisible to the three, eavesdrops on their talk and causes trouble amongst them by impersonating Trinculo's voice and interrupting Caliban when he speaks. Stephano, after repeated warnings to stop these catcalls, finally loses his patience and hits Trinculo several times. This passage is obviously intended as comic relief.

Caliban elaborates on his plan, describing how they can kill Prospero during his afternoon nap, and how Stephano could then have his beautiful daughter for his queen. He stresses how they must first destroy his magic books, ". . . for without them/He's but a sot, as I am, nor hath not/One spirit to command. They all do hate him/ As rootedly as I." The three agree to the plan.

Then Ariel plays a tune on his pipe, and when they comment on it, Caliban launches into a description of the strange music the island is full of. The three follow Ariel's music, promising that after finding its source they will resume their plan to kill Prospero.

Commentary

This scene is taken up where we left Caliban and the drunkards in Act II Scene 2, except by now all three are so drunk they are easily taunted into fighting with each other by the invisible Ariel. Their drunkenness and confusion makes this scene the funniest in the play, yet it is not without a certain point.

In the plot to murder Prospero, we can see a parody of Antonio and Sebastian's plot against Alonso. While Stephano and Trinculo agree to their scheme in an alcoholic haze, Antonio and Sebastian do so while blinded by greed and lust for power. Both plots are similarly planned to take advantage of a more powerful character while he is asleep and both are absurd, but for slightly different reasons: it must be obvious to Prospero that Caliban might try something of this nature, so his spirit-helpers must be put on alert during his nap to protect him — in the same way that Ariel was able to confront the treacherous courtiers' earlier attempt to kill Alonso.

The plot against Alonso is absurd because his kingdom is so far removed from the island. Killing the king in no way resolves the question of how to get back to Naples and take over his throne, which, in any case, will likely be filled with another ambitious interloper soon after the fleet returns with word of Alonso's and Ferdinand's supposed loss.

Shakespeare is using the parallels between the buffoonery of the drunkards, with their attempt to kill Prospero, and the treachery of Antonio and Sebastian, with their plot to depose Alonso, to make a general statement about desire for earthly power. A kingdom must fall to someone worthy of it, he seems to suggest, who will use its resources for good ends. Just wanting power like Antonio or Stephano is not enough, any more than Prospero's thirst for knowledge of magic was enough to sustain his entire life. Now that Prospero's occult knowledge is joined with his desire to direct worldly affairs, he is a complete and balanced person, well-suited to rule. Shakespeare hints that before Antonio or Stephano can inherit real responsibilities, they must similarly balance their desire for power with a sensitivity towards others and a moral vision that extends far beyond what theirs presently does.

Caliban continues to grow more complex. His paradoxical nature is well-illustrated in this scene: reeling from the murderous plot to a bittersweet memory of lost dreams, one minute he describes how to attack Prospero, "Batter his skull, or paunch him with a stake,/Or cut his wesand with thy knife," and the next he reminisces about a beautiful dream he once had, "The clouds methought would open and show riches/Ready to drop upon me, that, when I wak'd,/I cried to dream again."

His two sides are being revealed, his aggressive animal drives directed against Prospero and his instinctive appreciation for the natural wonders of the island, including Ariel's music — in short, the dual nature of Caliban as a "noble savage" is being presented. Even while drunk, he possesses a considerable intelligence, focusing on Prospero's nap time when he is vulnerable as well as the necessity for destroying his magic books to remove his power over his spiritual assistants. The alcohol has not changed Caliban like it has the other two, showing the natural resilience of the wild beast.

ACT III • SCENE 3

Summary

The king's courtiers, worn out from their long search, stop for a rest at the suggestion of Gonzalo, the oldest. Alonso admits that he no longer has any hope of finding his son alive. Antonio and Sebastian whisper to one another that now the others are so tired, they will not be so watchful, and they plot to kill them later that evening.

All at once, they hear strange music, and Prospero enters, invisibly, along with a procession of several strange beings, who carry in a banquet of food, perform a graceful dance, invite the men to eat, then disappear. Everyone expresses great amazement, Sebastian and Antonio even saying that now they will no longer doubt the incredible tales that travellers sometimes tell. But before they can start eating, there is a thunderclap, and Ariel enters in the shape of a harpy. This is a mythological symbol of revenge, a figure with the face of a woman and the body of a vulture. The banquet vanishes through some *"quaint device"* — perhaps a trapdoor in the stage. Ariel makes an accusing speech heard only by the three men, Alonso, Sebastian and Antonio.

When they try to draw their swords against Ariel, he says they may as well use them against the wind or try to stab the waves, as fight the forces of fate that brought them to the island to suffer their punishments for their wrongdoing in ousting Prospero and abandoning him on the sea. Alonso's son is dead, Ariel says, but this is only the beginning of their torments. Then he vanishes, and Prospero congratulates him on a fine performance. Meanwhile, the three guilty courtiers are distraught by this revelation and run off. Gonzalo, who has not heard the speech, but who assumes from Alonso's comments that their guilt has worked on them like a slow-acting poison, sends off the younger men to watch that they don't destroy themselves in this strange mood.

Commentary

Probably the most intriguing feature about this scene is the strange phrase, *"with a quaint device the banquet vanishes."* The question of how exactly this was staged has baffled generations of critics. One quite plausible explanation is offered by J.C. Adams: "the table (with the banquet) which rises does so on a trap upon which, concealed by the hangings of the table, there lurks a stagehand. Ariel descends from the heavens on a 'machine' (probably a rope-and-pulley device); he covers the banquet on the table with his harpy's wings; whereupon the stagehand removes a panel in the tabletop and whisks the banquet (usually a light refreshment) out of sight. Ariel then lifts his wings, and by a *"quaint device"* the banquet has indeed vanished."

No matter how it was actually staged, this matter of the disappearing banquet is the key to this scene. It is Prospero's test of the courtiers, and, by their reactions, he gauges the states of their morality. A temptation with food is not an idea that originated with Shakespeare: Eve was tempted with the apple, Essau traded his birthright for a "mess of pottage," and Christ was offered a banquet during his fast in the desert. These Biblical precedents heighten the moral seriousness of the test.

The banquet is an illusionary offering, just like the values the courtiers Alonso, Antonio and Sebastian are pursuing: power, nobility and fame. Being of little moral insight, they pursue the circumstance and outer appearance of these things, instead of their actual attainment. For instance, Sebastian and Antonio would kill Alonso for his kingdom — yet even if they did, they would not have gained it (being so far from Naples) but only an illusory grasp on it.

In this scene, Alonso at first hesitates to approach the banquet, perhaps fearing it may be poisoned. But he changes his mind and bids Antonio and Sebastian to join him in the feast. Yet it vanishes, and Ariel begins his accusing speech, which remains unheard by any except the three guilty men. Their swords are powerless against the elements that have swept them back to the island for their punishment for dethroning Prospero. In the guise of the harpy, or figure of revenge, Ariel announces that Alonso's son is indeed dead, but that their further penalties will include "Ling'ring perdition (worse than any death/can be at once) shall step by step attend/You and your ways." The three guilty men are confused and afraid and run off with their swords drawn.

Gonzalo, who has not heard Ariel's speech, assumes something close to the truth: "Their great guilt,/Like poison given to work a great time after,/Now gins to bite the spirits." Once again demonstrating his humanity, even to those who regularly mock him with their wit, Gonzalo sends out the younger men among the courtiers to find the guilty three and watch that they don't hurt themselves in their distracted states.

Notice how one scene in this act is devoted to each of the groups who washed up on the shore: first Ferdinand alone; then Stephano and Trinculo, in league with Caliban; and finally Antonio, Sebastian, Alonso, Gonzalo and the rest.

ACT IV • SCENE 1

Summary

Prospero has at last released Ferdinand from his labours and has recognized the affection between the young man and Miranda. Now he gives his blessing to their marriage, saying that Ferdinand will find Miranda well worth the trials he endured to prove his love for her. But he gives him a stern warning not to indulge in pre-marital sex.

Prospero then asks Ariel to provide some entertainment as his betrothal present to the happy couple. This takes place in the form of a masque, a popular courtly diversion in Shakespeare's time. Masques were mini-plays that consisted of songs, poetry recitations and dances by brightly costumed players, who often represented mythological characters. In this particular masque are Iris, the goddess of the rainbow; Juno, wife of Jupiter and queen of the gods, who protects the sanctity of marriage and the health of women in childbirth; and Ceres, an earth-goddess who bestows this blessing on the young couple:

> Vines with clust'ring bunches growing,
> Plants with goodly burden bowing . . . .
> Scarcity and want shall shun you;
> Ceres' blessing so is on you.
>
> (Act IV, Sc. 1, 112-17)

But towards the end of one dance featuring the figures of straw-hatted reapers, Prospero recalls Caliban's plot and ends the pageant abruptly.

This startles the young couple a great deal, and Miranda comments that she has never seen her father so angry. Prospero apologizes with a stirring piece of poetry, one of the most famous from this play:

> Our revels now are ended . . . . We are such stuff
> As dreams are made on, and our little life
> Is rounded with a sleep.
>
> (Act IV, Sc. 1, 148-58)

Prospero asks Ariel how he left the three drunkards, and Ariel replies they were so drunk that they were striking the air and beating the ground. He had led them with his song through briars and prickly shrubs and into a slime-covered pond behind Prospero's cave. Prospero asks Ariel to fetch some cheap, colourful clothes and hang them on a line to distract the three when they approach.

Soon Caliban, Stephano and Trinculo enter, soaking, smelly and cross from their ordeal, and spot the bright clothes. Caliban is frantic with impatience to get on with the murder of Prospero, but the other two stop at the clothes, arguing who will get which and taking one after another down from the line.

Prospero eventually puts an end to their rummaging by unleashing spirits in the form of hounds who quickly chase all three away. Prospero adds a final curse of "dry convulsions" and "aged cramps" as they flee.

Commentary

Prospero is now sure that Ferdinand, having stood his trials uncomplainingly, is worthy of his daughter. In fact, Ferdinand is the only one among the courtiers who seems to have grasped the true nature of this testing by Prospero, thus demonstrating his moral superiority. He is also the only courtier who comes close to deciphering the strange music and the other unusual activities that occur on the island. Almost as soon as he heard Ariel's music in Act I Scene 2, he guessed it had a supernatural origin. In the present scene, watching the masque, he asks Prospero, "May I be bold/To think these spirits?" His sensitivity to the spirit world, coupled with what we are shown of his ability to cope with practical matters, make him a suitable son-in-law for Prospero. His positive nature is also revealed by his complete acceptance of his father-in-law and the island's setting when he declares:

> . . . Let me live here ever!
> So rare a wond'red father and a wise
> Makes this place Paradise.

(Act IV, Sc. 1, 122-24)

No one else among the courtiers except Gonzalo has spoken in any such glowing terms about the island.

With Ferdinand such a worthy partner for Miranda, why does Prospero issue such a harsh and repeated directive not to tamper with her virginity until they are safely married, under the dire curse that if he does, the couple will come to hate each other? One answer might be that Prospero is her father, careful of her suitors, and eager to chaperone her possessively. Perhaps he is saying this as a final test for Ferdinand, never content to take anyone's good intentions for granted. But this is not the whole answer. Remember that Prospero is more than just Miranda's father and teacher. He is the source of all civil authority on the island, its "king" as much as it has one. He is also the island's moral and religious leader, its "priest" as much as it has one. His entire role during the play has been to offer moral instruction to the court party, by placing them into trying or tempting circumstances and letting them decide how best to act. In this way, he has taken on the role of a god, of a higher creative intelligence in whose hands are the lives of lower beings. These exercises have tended to divide people into several groups — and of all the characters, Caliban is the most direct contrast to Ferdinand. Both have had the same toil, of carrying wood; both have felt an attraction for Miranda; and both are sensitive to the island's world of spirits. Yet each has responded in a very different manner: Ferdinand with his gift of reason, self-control and imagination, Caliban with his instinctive aggression, self-abandon and fear. Prospero's stern warning to Ferdinand seems to be caused by this contrast —

"don't be like Caliban," he is saying — and by the need for the marriage rites to take place before man and women can be considered mates in the eyes of both the civilized world and the highest moral authority.

The Tempest, unlike many of Shakespeare's plays, seems quite concerned with marriage. Instead of having the young couple united in the very last scene of the play, here the playwright has them matched up and enjoying a celebration of their betrothal by the fourth act. This masque seems to consume an inordinate amount of time, until one remembers that this play was in fact written and performed to honour the marriage of King James' daughter to a German ruler. The masque, complete with blessings by the appropriate goddesses, spoke directly to the stately engaged couple, who saw its performance at court. Even the goddesses who appeared in the masque were carefully chosen — Venus and her son Cupid being specifically excluded, probably because their natures as the figures of passionate physical love would contrat too much with Prospero's warnings. Or perhaps Shakespeare had a feeling that this royal marriage was one of political convenience rather than passion and was making an appropriate comment. In any case, the goddesses that do appear promise prosperity and fertility, quite acceptable blesssings on a royal couple.

One of the play's most well-known lines is contained in this scene, in Prospero's speech after he ends the masque: "We are such stuff/As dreams are made on." This entire speech is fine poetry, perhaps the best in the play. It used to be the custom among some critics to view *The Tempest* as Shakespeare's final play, in which he deliberately uttered his goodbyes to the world of the stage. This speech was cited as one of several from the play to support this assertion, referring as it does to "the great globe itself," or Shakespeare's home theater for many years, the Globe. Now it is generally agreed that Shakespeare wrote all or part of one other play, *Henry VIII*, after *The Tempest*, and the weight of this interpretation has been lifted from this and several other similar speeches in this play.

However, another troubling point occurs in this scene: how did Prospero come to forget about the murderous plot of Caliban and his drunken company? This may be a mere staging technique to keep the action rolling, a good excuse to chop off the uninspiring spectacle of the masque. It may be a deliberate device to try to make the audience believe that the play's ending is somehow not pre-ordained, to encourage their interest in the prospect of a tremendous battle shaping up between Prospero, Caliban and the other courtiers.

Then again, the playwright may be offering final proof that even with the happiest of all excuses for being distracted — his daughter's engagement — Prospero will never again lose sight of his pressing concerns. His anger flares at the recent betrayals of Caliban and the more distant treachery of Antonio, and he vows to set things right. This transition from the happiness of the betrothal to the evil presence in the play is necessary before the final curtain can fall.

The outsmarting of the drunkards turns out to be no more difficult than hanging out some bright clothes to distract them. They come on the scene, considerably deflated by the loss of their bottle and their recent ordeals in the pond. After losing sight of the goal of killing Prospero once already (when they followed Ariel's music through the bushes and into the pond), Stephano and Trinculo dismiss it a second time while they pick up all the cheap clothes they wish, showing their utter lack of self-control and inner vision. If they had any sense of priorities whatsoever, they would have killed Prospero first, so that with him gone, the clothes and everything else on the island would be theirs. Even Caliban grasps this but cannot steer them away from their rummaging. In this way, they fail the simple test that Prospero has set for them. The punishment of the three has been appropriate for those of such unworthy characters — physical torment in the underbrush and fouling in a pond — and Prospero does not bother to vanquish them with anything more elevated than spirits in the form of dogs, who chase them away. Trinculo and Stephano, the supposed representatives of civilization, show themselves as completely lacking vision and inner worth; while Caliban, for all his treachery, has for once tried to persevere through a difficult project, showing some small amount of self-control and rational insight beginning to emerge, even if his ends at the moment are typically aggressive and destructive.

ACT V • SCENE 1

Summary

Prospero says the time has come for him to finish up his project. He asks Ariel how the courtiers are, and the spirit replies that they are all frozen in place in distorted and mournful poses, forming a scene so touching that a human would feel sorry for them. Prospero replies that he will take pity on them:

> Though with their high wrongs I am struck to th' quick
> Yet with my nobler reason 'gainst my fury
> Do I take part. The rarer action is
> In virtue than in vengeance . . . .
>
> (Act V, Sc. 1, 25-28)

He sends Ariel to release them from the charm and bring them back, so he can restore them to their right minds. Then, in a soliloquy, he speaks about the kinds of things he has done with his magic and says that he is now about to give it up. He declares that he will bury his wand in the earth and throw his magic book into the sea.

Ariel returns with the courtiers and stands them inside a charmed circle, where Prospero gradually brings them out of their induced sleep. He takes off his magic robe and dresses so they will recognize him as the Duke of Milan. As they awake, he reveals his identity to them. Alonso quickly offers his dukedom back to him and asks his forgiveness. Prospero greets Gonzalo warmly but tells Antonio and Sebastian in an aside that he could expose them for their treacherous plans against the king. He says he won't this time and will even forgive Antonio for his crime against him, but he demands that they also recognize his right to reclaim his dukedom.

As a final twist, Prospero says he has lost his daughter just as Alonso lost his son during the recent tempest. Alonso says he wishes that their two children were living in Naples as the king and queen. With that, Prospero reveals Ferdinand and Miranda in his cave playing chess. Ferdinand says he chose Miranda for his wife while his father was absent and presumed dead, but Alonso gives his instant approval to the match.

Then Ariel returns with the ship's master and the boatswain, who explain that the ship and all its crew are completely safe in a harbour nearby. Next, Ariel brings in Caliban, Stephano and Trinculo, the latter two still wearing their stolen clothes. All three are feeling much the worse for wear. Caliban asks for pardon, saying, "What a thrice-double ass / Was I, to take this drunkard for a god/And worship this dull fool!" and declaring, "I'll be wise hereafter,/And seek for grace."

Prospero orders Caliban to go back to his cell and decorate it, and Alonso tells the other two to go and put the stolen clothes back where they found them. Prospero invites the whole company to spend the evening with him in his cave, while he retells everything that has happened. As a final command to Ariel, Prospero asks for calm seas and favourable winds on their sail back to Naples, after which he may have his freedom.

Prospero offers an epilogue, saying that since he now has no more magic charms, the audience must by their applause release him from the island and with their cheers fill out the sails on his homeward trip to Naples.

Commentary

In this concluding scene, all the various groups of characters are brought together at Prospero's command for a final resolution. Each character that has faced a test is judged according to the correctness of his response, then punished or rewarded accordingly. Prospero is conscious of the time passing by and accomplishes all this with great efficiency.

First, he brings in the court party. When Ariel tells him of their appearance and how if he were human he would pity them, Prospero is moved to agree. Although he is now in a position to torture or destroy his enemies, he chooses the higher path of forgiveness, saying, "The rarer action is/In virtue than in vengeance." This follows a pattern existing in Shakespeare's comedies and romances, and it especially recalls Portia's "quality of mercy" speech in *The Merchant of Venice*. When Prospero reveals his true identity to the courtiers, Alonso responds immediately by asking his forgiveness. Prospero has to speak differently to Antonio and Sebastian, threatening that although he knows about their recent plot, he will not reveal it if they agree to restore his dukedom to him. It is hard to say whether these two men are at all repentant, or merely forced into submission by Prospero's superior strength. In either case, they have something to think about and may even decide to change their ways. Prospero does call Antonio and Sebastian "unnatural" at one point, harkening back to the earlier commentary about Gonzalo's Utopia and the "noble savage" idea. These two are unnatural, yes, the products of a civilized world, but, at the same time, they lack moral strength or real values to guide them through life. Their negative presence is an argument for the "noble savage's" superiority over civilized man.

But this brings us around again to Caliban, who is seen in an uncharacteristic light in this final scene. Perhaps for fear of punishment, or else from real understanding of his own nature, Caliban declares that he will from this point on "be wise hereafter/And seek for grace." If true, this will remove him from the category of the "noble savage," for when Caliban's animal nature willingly submits to the leash of reason, he starts to become a civilized being.

It has been said that all those capable of redeeming themselves find redemption in *The Tempest*. The benefit of the doubt cannot be given to Antonio, Sebastian or the drunken clowns, Stephano and Trinculo, who are assuredly the unworthy dregs of humanity. But it may perhaps be extended to Caliban, who after all, seems to be on his way now to Europe with the rest of the group — or perhaps Prospero will return him to his freedom on the island, or even offer him a choice whether to stay behind or accompany them. Faced with such a choice, it is intriguing to speculate which aspect of his nature, the "noble" or the "savage," Caliban would then act out. Without knowing for certain which way Caliban, Antonio and Sebastian will go, it is difficult to completely resolve the "civilization versus nature" debate, since no definite equation of worth between these characters can be produced.

The characters of Ferdinand and Miranda continue to be shown as blemish-free; Ferdinand for succeeding at his difficult trial — the only one of the court party to do so — and Miranda for her continued innocence. Miranda's exclamation on seeing the rest of the courtiers, "How beautuous mankind is! O brave new world/That has such people in't!", gave Aldous Huxley the ironic title for his novel, *Brave New*

World, one of the most well-known of all anti-Utopian books. Prospero's reply, "'Tis new to thee," reveals his weariness with the world, amplified later in the scene when he says that upon his return to Milan, his every third thought will be on the grave. This also echoes his previous statement to Ferdinand, when giving him Miranda's hand, that he is giving him a third of his life. All these statements, as well as his earlier decision to give up his practice of magic, show how relieved Prospero is to be removed from the position he has occupied during the play — supreme moral authority and stage-manager for everything that has gone on across the whole island.

Gonzalo serves to summarize much of the play's action in this scene, wishing a hearty blessing to the young couple, and recalling his joke in the opening scene as the boatswain and others reappear. This reminds the audience of the play's title and the storm that initiated all the action they have just viewed.

The fundamental imagery of the sea and the tempest are shown in different terms now. Remember that Iris, goddess of the rainbow, was present at the masque. This suggested the peace after the storm. In this scene, after the reunion with his father, Ferdinand is moved to say, "Though the seas threaten, they are merciful./I have curs'd them without cause." It was the upheaval of the tempest that caused the courtiers to come to the island, and now that it's over, everyone has benefitted: Ferdinand and Miranda have found each other; Prospero has regained his former dukedom, Alonso's burden of guilt has been removed, and a historic new union between their families is about to occur. The courtiers, Antonio and Sebastian, have had, at the very least, an adventure that will make great tales and have, at best, gained a valuable moral insight. Caliban has perhaps seen the way to a more balanced existence through discipline and submission, the drunkards, Stephano and Trinculo, have been harmlessly humiliated, and Gonzalo has been congratulated for his continuing human warmth. When Prospero has Ariel promise "calm seas, auspicious gales" and a trip so quick that they catch up to the other ships in the fleet on their way back to Naples, he is putting all mention of the tempest behind him and is signifying that the work he started with its rough waters has been completely finished and has led to a time of complete calm.

Character Sketches
Prospero

Prospero is derived from the Latin pro, forward, before, and spero, I hope, and thus it means hopefully looking forward, a most suitable epithet for him. In Act I, Sc. 2, 155, he claims that fortitude, inspired by Miranda's smiles, "raised in me an undergoing stomach, to bear up against what should ensue."

Liberal arts is the name he gives his studies, including more than magic alone, for his reputation for learning was "without a parallel", Act I, Sc. 2, 74. The books given him by Gonzalo were volumes that he prized above his dukedom, his confession that he preferred study to governing his state. On the island he devoted the afternoons to his studies. We are told only of the results of his studies, nothing about his methods. His investigations were all for benevolent purposes. With his magic he freed Ariel, taught speech to Caliban, knew of the presence of the Neapolitan ship, and raised the storm to drive it ashore. Although he could not make himself invisible, he instructed Ariel to do so, or to take the shape of a harpy. Prospero, through Ariel, could summon goddesses, spirits, nymphs, fairies, and reapers, make spirits take the form of dogs, and create a magic circle for his victims. The tools or symbols of his profession are a magic robe, a wand, and his book. He wears his robe and carries his wand during the performance of his magic, but discards them to resume his natural powers. His robe does not make him invisible, but it hides his personality. The courtiers could not recognize him until after he has "discased" himself. Magicians were divided into two classes, those who command the services of supernatural beings, as Prospero does, and those who have leagued themselves with the devil, as the witches in *Macbeth*.

He believes in the beauty of the world and mankind, as expressed by Miranda. A smiling face assures him that all is well, Act I, Sc. 2, 153. He considers life to be like a dream, beginning and ending with a sleep, with the unknown, "our little life is rounded out in sleep," Act IV, Sc. 1, 125. "Every third thought shall be my grave," Act V, Sc. 1, 312, indicates his attitude towards death.

Although the characters of the participants have little chance of development within four hours, we find certain changes derived from Prospero's story of his life, as told to Miranda in Act I, Sc. 2. His twelve years on the island have made him a different man. He was an excellent ruler with the reputation of being the first among the Italian princes. His chief pursuit was his "secret" studies, that is, his delving into the secrets of the supernatural. This blinded his penetration into the natural, and he failed to recognize the villainy in others. He held himself aloof from the world and too readily offered the duties of the state to his brother. His mistaken generosity led to his downfall, his nemesis.

His Milan betrayal opened his eyes to the need of a proper understanding of people, and the contrast between Gonzalo's kindness and Antonio's villainy draws his attention to underlying motives in human beings. He boldly accuses all his former enemies of their crimes, distinguishes his benefactors from his opponents, and punishes or rewards each according to his deserts. He is stern with Ferdinand in testing his merits and sincerity, dominates Antonio and Sebastian by revealing his knowledge of their treachery, and degrades Stephano and Trinculo by making them as filthy as their drunkenness. In his suspicions he exercises his magic as a test to bring out all the qualities of the courtiers. He enforces obedience of Caliban, Ariel, Ferdinand, and the crew and passengers of the ship. His manner is always dignified, and he is imperial and impartial in his justice.

He loved his brother before the betrayal as much as his own life and overlooked his gradual assumption of power. His affection for Miranda was absolute. His sympathy set Ariel free from his cruel imprisonment, though he was again stern in threatening him with worse if he disobeyed. Though he forced him to serve him, he showered upon him terms of endearment, My Ariel, My trickey spirit, My quaint Ariel, My dainty Ariel, My diligence, etc. His regard for and gratitude to Gonzalo are climaxed in his embracing him on revealing himself to him. His kindness to Caliban extended to offering him to share his home with him and teaching him the use of language and training him to human decency. His kindness ended only after the monster's evidence of brutishness.

His apparent harshness, when displayed, was not in angry passion, but rather an evidence of his good judgment. He reduced Caliban to a position in which he could do no harm. He made Ferdinand do menial work to test his worthiness. He recognizes the lack of conscience and unchanged nature of Antonio, but is content with depriving him of his usurped dukedom and inflicting on him more pains than on Sebastian. He assists Ariel in setting the dogs on Stephano and Trinculo and Caliban, knowing that their low natures can be penetrated only by physical discomfort and pain. He feels that perhaps he is imposing too much on Ariel's willingness to assist him, and he softens his hardness by promising him early release.

That he was spirited to the point of anger against injustice shows in denunciations of his enemies to Miranda in the second scene. His anger against Caliban for his insult to Miranda is the most striking example. He has not a kind word for him, reduces him to practical slavery and punishes him with pinching and cramping pains, but in the end he restores him to household services. He pretended anger with Ferdinand when the latter refused to serve him and drew his sword against him over the insult, but, secure in his magic power, he disarmed him and made him submissive. He grows angry when he witnesses the planning of the murder of Alonso and when he hears from Ariel the plot of Caliban and the drunken butler and jester to kill him, seize Miranda, and take possession of the island.

Though he had the power to destroy all those who plotted against him, his kindness of heart prevailed, for he recognized that "the rarer action is in virtue than in vengeance," Act V, Sc. 1, 27. He appreciates the completeness of Alonso's change of heart and entirely forgets the past wrongs. Sebastian and Antonio cannot be wholly forgiven because of their continuance of hardness of heart. Stephano and Trinculo are allowed to return to their places in the court, but Caliban, who can do no further mischief after the return of the rest to Naples, is left in full enjoyment of his island.

Summary

Summing up the character of Prospero, we find him intellectually great, the possessor of rare spiritual powers, a statesman, dignified, affectionate, stern and severe when necessary, grateful, considerate, philosophic, and with a serene outlook on life.

Miranda

She is generally regarded as the finest among all the women created by Shakespeare, the type of what he regarded as a perfect woman unspoiled by social customs and conventionalities. She has had no contact since her babyhood with men or women, except her reserved and studious father, who has trained her in all essential needs of life, speech, dress, gentleness, obedience, and modesty. She was under three when she left Milan, and her only recollection of social life is that of women in attendance on her. She is totally unaware of her status in life and of the world in general. So far as she knows all the world consists of herself and her father and the strange creature Caliban who waits on them. She is probably unaware of the existence of Ariel, for her father puts her to sleep before the spirit comes at his call. She is fifteen when her father first reveals their past life to her. Her age appears to us more slowly maturing northerners as being too early for her quite evident maturity, but in Italy women at fifteen are as ready for marriage as at nineteen or twenty with us. Juliet, in the play, *Romeo and Juliet*, was fourteen.

Miranda's name, like that of Prospero, is taken from the Latin, the present participle of the verb mirari, mirandus, to admire or to wonder, and means literally the admired one. Ferdinand, in the love scene opening Act III, when he asks her her name, breaks out in exclamations as to its suitability for her, "Admired Miranda! Indeed the top of admiration!" And, as we proceed in the story, we agree with him that she is a source of wonder and admiration.

There is mentioned in the play as to her personal appearance, the colour of her eyes and hair, her stature, her bearing. We depend on the effect that she produces on others, on her actions and speech. The first impression that she makes on Ferdinand leads him to call her a goddess, and immediately we picture to ourselves the sculptured forms of Venus and Juno. Alonso also terms her a goddess when he first meets her, Act V, Sc. 1, 187, and when Caliban tempts Stephano with her as a wife, he states that her beauty is her most important characteristic and that she is beyond comparison with any other woman, Act III, Sc. 2, 96.

She is filled with grief over the supposed drowning of the passengers on the ship, among whom there surely must be some worthy creature, an oracular or mysterious prophecy, which was to be filled in a manner she little expected. Her heart ached to think of the sufferings her father must have endured when he was cast adrift in a "rotten butt". She was moved to tears of gratitude over the kindness of Gonzalo in providing for their future. Her pity for Ferdinand's hard and menial task led her to try to take the wood from him and pile it herself, and she did her utmost to induce her father to relent in his supposed harshness. Her sympathy led her to her first disobedience of her father's commands. Her sensitive nature as a woman led her to tears under excess of gladness or sorrow.

Her father's revelation of their rank and the existence of other people and the good and bad in them has awakened her womanhood, has opened her eyes to the tree of knowledge, just as Eve's were opened, but so differently, by the serpent. Fortunately Ferdinand was the first man for her to see, the upright and cultured prince, and her whole being flowed out to him. Her next acquaintance was the court of Naples with the same appearance and dress as Ferdinand, and she exclaimed on the beauty of men and the goodly world that produced such. Work was simply an obligation that comes to all, undivided in nature by our conventions of menial and white-collar distinctions. The piling of the wood became necessary because of her father's law, and it made no difference whether a man or a woman did it. Her disobedience to her father revealing her name to Ferdinand and in meeting him secretly resulted from the conflict between duty and sympathy, and instinctively she chose the latter.

In her innocence of the regulations of society and her native spontaneity her whole heart goes out to Ferdinand at first sight. She has now attained womanhood, and naturally her entire being calls for a mate. She sees in Ferdinand all that is necessary to fill out her life, and she frankly asks him if he loves her. To her, love and service in love are the same thing, and if he does not want her as his wife, she will gladly become his servant. His acceptance of her as wife is gratefully acknowledged, but not much more than that. She would be equally grateful merely to serve him, and she immediately leaves him after the avowal. Her response is vastly different from the swooning happiness of Portia after Bassanio's success in selecting the right casket in *The Merchant of Venice*. But her love is steadfast and serene, and the emotions of both are so well controlled that they are next found settled down at a game of chess.

Summary

Miranda is goddesslike in beauty and bearing, innocent, unsophisticated, direct in speech and action, compassionate, womanly, self-controlled, and frankly spontaneous.

Ferdinand

He is the only son and heir of King Alonso and consequently has been educated and trained as a prince. He has accompanied his father and the

Neapolitan court to the marriage of his sister Claribel to the king of Tunis, was wrecked on the island, jumped into the sea and swam ashore, believing himself to be the only survivor. As he tells us of his past life, he has appreciated the beauty of many ladies, been charmed with their conversation, and liked many of them for their virtue, but he has found in each of them some defect to offset the perfection of her character. We are told nothing directly as to his personal appearance. But Prospero calls him a "goodly" person, and Miranda thinks him a "thing divine" and noble. He states that he is the best of all that speak the Italian tongue, Act I, Sc. 2, 423. He is inclined to be religious. He wants to know Miranda's name for his prayers.

When Prospero charges him with being a spy and threatens to put him in chains and make him his slave, his dignity and sense of justice make him defiant. He draws his sword to challenge his accuser, and is prevented from fighting only by the exercise of Prospero's magic. He cannot understand why his arm is powerless and attributes it to his state of mind troubled over the loss of his father and all the court and with the shock of the wreck and his own narrow escape from drowning. In the love scene opening Act III he is shocked at the thought of a woman's piling wood, and he refuses to let Miranda help him. He defends himself charmingly when he explains to his father his betrothal to Miranda.

His grief over the loss of his father is immediately forgotten for the time being with his first sight of Miranda and he falls at once in love with her. He compares her with the ladies of his court and finds no defect in her, even though he is unaware that her social rank equals his own. He is ready to abandon his right to the crown of Naples and to remain on the island with Miranda and his new-found father.

Summary

He is noble, courtly, spirited, intelligent, direct in speech, inclined to be religious, and gives promise of being a good king. We really know little about him, for he appears on the stage on only four occasions. He does not impress us as being a strong man of action, as do most of the other characters. We are inclined to think that Miranda is worthy of a greater husband.

Antonio

He is the younger brother of Prospero, and if the latter is an old man, he is probably nearly as old, although we take him to be young in his activities. Prospero had full faith in his trustworthiness and loyalty in appointing him to the regency of Milan, which he carried out capably for a time. But as his influence and power grew, he first won over the state counsellors to his views, then appropriated to his own use the duchy's revenues, and finally entered into a treasonable alliance with Alonso, king of Naples to dethrone and destroy Prospero. In return Milan was to become a fief of Naples and pay the usual feudal fees, and attend the lord's court. The Neapolitan army was admitted into the gates of Milan, Prospero and his daughter were seized, and Gonzalo instructed to set them adrift on the Mediterranean. Antonio, in attendance upon Alonso, accompanied him and his court to Tunis to celebrate the marriage of Claribel to the king of that country. Thus he is present in the shipwreck to fall under the magic of Prospero.

A curious error or oversight on the part of the author is evident in a speech of Ferdinand, Act I, Sc. 2, 430, where he says that the Duke of Milan and his brave (fine) son were lost in the wreck. There is no further mention of this son in the play, and we learn later that no one has been drowned. If he had a son worth naming, especially when he is characterized as fine or noble, why does he have no part in the play? Shakespeare may have intended to use him as he did Adrian and Francisco, but simply forgot about the remark.

In his dealings with his fellow courtiers in the opening scene of Act II, he ridicules Gonzalo, flippantly suggests a bet over which of them will laugh first, sneers at the island, and makes himself generally offensive. He is sceptical over all the supernatural occurrences, indicating an absence of the spiritual or emotional side of his character, and therefore irreligious. He declares that he has never been troubled with a conscience, whose pricks are no more to him than a chilblain, and he mocks Sebastian for considering such a thing.

The experience he has had in Milan in winning men to his interests serves him well in seducing Sebastian into a conspiracy against Alonso. We are not told his motive, but we gather that he foresaw the restoration of the freedom of Milan by making Sebastian king of Naples. Sebastian has no thought of such a happening, and we note Antonio's well-planned method to bring it about. The opportunity comes when Ariel's music puts them all asleep, except the two. After a brief discussion of the cause of their sleepiness, Antonio breaks off with hesitating words, "What might . . . What might . . .", leaving his thought unfinished and securing Sebastian's full attention. In flattery he praises him and sets him wondering by telling him that he is asleep to his opportunity for great things. He sees something of high importance and sets him wondering by telling him that he is blind to his opportunity, that he is on the high road to a greatness that he does not realize. Then, after beating about the bush for a while, he reminds him that Ferdinand has been drowned, that Claribel, the next heir, is so far away that she is as good as dead, and that therefore Sebastian is the heir. He tells him that he is as fully competent as Gonzalo or any of the other lords. Then he reminds him of his own success in securing Milan for himself. But Sebastian has a conscience that troubles him. Antonio ridicules conscience, and he points out opportune is the present time. Alonso is asleep and at their mercy. Three inches of steel will put an end to him, and when it is done the lords will accept him as readily as a cat laps up milk. Sebastian is at last won over and directs Antonio to strike the blow. But when the latter requires that they both strike together, Sebastian draws him aside to discuss this new aspect, and while they converse together Ariel rouses the sleepers and their attempt is foiled.

We do not know how long he held the rule of Milan before his first crime, but it was long enough to train him in iniquity. Its planning must have been deliberate, not a sudden passion to overtake him, and therefore was all the more reprehensible. This explains his contempt of conscience, which must have often been thrust aside. His crime was followed by twelve years of success to prove that he was justified in its perpetration. He has used every device of his fertile mind to make Sebastian a fellow criminal. And when the first attempt to carry it out fails, he spurs him on again at the first opportunity to a second attempt. Then in the final scene, when Prospero charges him with his past sins, he shows, absolutely no remorse nor even regret. His heart is completely hardened.

His punishment at first appears light to us, limited to the loss of his usurped power and the infliction of physical pain when the rightful penalty was death. But he would probably suffer more in the humiliation of his disgrace and loss of power during the remainder of his life.

Summary

We find this villain of the play unscrupulous, crafty, sneering and contemptuous, without conscience, unrepentant, unsympathetic, irreligious, and without one redeeming quality.

Alonso

He is the king of Naples, probably forty or fifty years old, with a son, Ferdinand, a daughter, Claribel, and a brother, Sebastian. While there is no evidence of his desire to subdue Milan, history tells that the two states were enemies and sometimes at war with each other. Naples, which comprised all southern Italy, was rather a country than a city state, and was of considerable importance in the middle ages. Milan, next to Venice and Genoa, was the leading city state of northern Italy, and Antonio's offer of its subjection was a strong temptation to Alonso, and naturally he took advantage of it. No explanation beyond that of the low regard in which life was held at the time, and is still in eastern Europe, can be made of his cruelty in ordering the death of Prospero and Miranda. He is twice accused of this cruelty, once by Ariel at the time of the proffered banquet, Act III, Sc. 3, 72, and the other by Prospero as he stood within the magic circle, Act V, Sc. 1, 71.

In general opinion of the time he would be ranked high as king of an important country. His court, with the exception of Gonzalo, consists of feeble nobles. He had disregarded their advice not to marry Claribel to a Moorish monarch, a decision that resulted in their shipwreck and an opportunity for the conspirators to kill him. At all times they pay little attention to him. He had entrusted Gonzalo with the task of disposing of Prospero and his daughter and apparently knew nothing of its failure. He does not appear to be either a wise or a powerful ruler.

His sincere love for his son and his daughter indicates the best in his character. He believed that he was acting for the best in marrying Claribel to the king of Tunis. He afterwards regretted the marriage, for he believed that it resulted in the loss of both of his children. His grief over the supposed drowning of his son was so deep that he could not be appeased by the efforts of Gonzalo and the others to divert him, and he declared his intention to drown himself. His reunion with his son at the close of the play and acceptance of Miranda as a daughter bring him complete happiness again. The intensity of his feelings is shown in the shock of his son's loss. None of his courtiers, except Gonzalo, shows any sympathy for him. Indeed, they rather blame him for the disaster they have all suffered. Their attempts at humour are probably intended to divert his attention, but the nature of their wit seems to contradict such a purpose. He pays no attention to them except to bid them cease their chattering. He is roused only when Gonzalo refers to the expedition to Tunis, which only rouses his grief again.

The disaster of the wreck is a nemesis for the crime of Milan. It has a direct bearing on it after a period of twelve years. He brought it more directly on himself by his error of judgment in marrying Claribel out of her country. His present sufferings are so intense that they soon turn to remorse and lead to his complete forgiveness of Prospero. In his excess of emotion he overlooks his kingly right in choosing a wife for his son. Her destiny to become queen of Naples atones in full for his crime against Milan.

Summary

Though cruel at first, he redeems himself later. He becomes tender hearted, repentant, appreciative, generous, and grateful. He is not a good judge of character in surrounding himself with courtiers and shows little suitability as a king. In all there is little more to be said about him than about any other man in misfortune.

Sebastian

He is the only brother of Alonso and heir to the throne in case of the death of the king's two children. In character and action he is stronger, though more wicked, than his brother, but not to a great extent. Alonso and Sebastian, and Prospero and Antonio are parallel pairs and the extremes of good and evil in the latter are reflected in a less degree in the former.

Nowhere does he make an effort to advise or console Alonso. On the contrary, he accuses Alonso as responsible for the disaster, "You may thank yourself for this great loss," Act II, Sc. 1, 12. He ridicules Gonzalo's remarks with scorn, sarcasm, and mockery, and he makes sport of the minor lords. This scornful treatment of his equals in social standing is one of the outlets of an evil mind and reveals a sense of inferiority which cannot cope with good in others. Beyond his speech of accusation against his brother, he has not a single idea of importance to contribute to the conversation until he is alone with Antonio. In Act II, Sc. 1, 219, he confesses that he is indolent by birth, "To ebb hereditary sloth instructs me."

He has had no thought of seizing the government until Antonio prompts him to it. When the latter takes advantage of the others being asleep and talks seriously to him, he changes his bantering into serious speech. He has thought only of Claribel's right to the throne in case of Ferdinand's death. Then as Antonio unfolds his design, his sense of right and wrong leads him to speak of qualms of conscience, which Antonio soon overrides. After he finally agrees to the murder of Alonso, he hesitates to strike the victim jointly with Antonio, and this hesitation leads to the temporary frustration of the plot. Then before the banquet, when the court is again assembled and the courtiers are exhausted with their tramping over the island, it is Antonio who brings up the plot again, and Sebastian affirms that they will carry it through this time. We note that on both occasions it is Prospero who prepares the opportunity for them, purposely to reveal the rascality of the two.

Ariel's music, which charms the others to sleep, has no effect on either Antonio or Sebastian. The Shapes which bring in the banquet merely remind him of the tales of foreign monsters told by travellers. His only interest is in the banquet itself. And when Ariel as a harpy causes it to disappear, he and Antonio draw their swords, and they repeat the performance and run after the Shapes when they carry out the table. We are told that he stands charmed in the magic circle, and he certainly has nothing to say until Prospero reveals the proposed crime against Alonso. He thinks that the devil must be at work to reveal such a secret. The production of Ferdinand and Miranda at chess he declares sarcastically "a most high miracle!" His sneers continue again with the appearance of the drunken butler and jester.

Like Antonio, he shows no trace of repentance, even when faced with his crime. He has no headship of the state to lose, but Prospero's threatened withholding of exposure will hang over him for the rest of his life. But like his friend he will have suffering, "Thou'rt pinch'd for it now, Sebastian," Act V, Sc. 1, 74.

Summary

He is sneering, sarcastic, mocking, lacking in initiative in crime, but ready to participate in it, ridicules the supernatural, and is unrepentant to the end. Though he speaks of a conscience, he is ready to discard it. There is no doubt as to his fearlessness; he is always ready to draw his sword, even against the spirit world. Antonio is the promoter, Sebastian the follower in crime.

Gonzalo

He is the bright light both of the play and of the court of Naples. His importance is to offer relief in serious situations and to draw to our attention the characters of the other courtiers. His description in the dramatis personae, an honest old counsellor, estimates him fully in a few words. He is the only loyal follower of the king in all the court, quite garrulous, as old people sometimes are, and is inclined to be philosophic.

Though he was subject to Alonso's commands and found it to his duty to dispose of Antonio, the tenderness of his heart was shocked at the cruelty of the order, which meant slow death to the victims. His supplying Prospero even with his well loved books is suggestive of his foresight and of his tribute to the culture of the duke. In the height of the storm about to wreck the ship he recognizes the skill and assuredness of the Boatswain and finds comfort for his fellow courtiers in assuring them that they will not be drowned, humorously suggesting that the man who is born to be hanged will never be drowned. When they are safely ashore it becomes his duty to bid them all be grateful for the sparing of their lives. Later when Alonso realizes that his son is missing, he is the only courtier who tries to console their king and he chides the others for their thoughtless cruelty, "You rub the sore when you should bring the plaster," Act II, Sc. 1, 134. Antonio acknowledges the goodness of Gonzalo and urges that his death be linked with that of Alonso, Act II, Sc. 1, 282.

His grim humour in trying to make the best of a bad situation is early shown in saying, referring to the Boatswain that a man born to be hanged will never be drowned, and at the apparent immediate crashing of the ship that he would give a thousand furlongs of sea for an acre of dry land. He puns on the words dolour and dollar, Act II, Sc. 1, 19. He finally distracts their attention from pure nonsense to his description of the impossible Utopia he would make of the island. On the return of the mariners in the closing scene he teases the Boatswain on his not being drowned and on his omission of blasphemy from his speech.

His greatness is most fully found in the intention of Antonio to kill him along with Alonso, referred to above, for he would be the only one of the court who would oppose them after the murder. Gonzalo's first thought was to comfort his king in his loss. The very fact of their escape from death is a much greater reason for thankfulness. If they had been drowned there would be much grief at their homes. At the time of the plot against Alonso he senses danger to his king and warns him after he wakens and sees the drawn swords in the hands of Antonio and Sebastian. He bids Alonso not to fear to partake of the banquet, knowing that he needs food. He warns him a second time of the danger threatening him, Act III, Sc. 3, 106. In the stage direction of Act V, Sc. 1, 58, we note that Alonso is attended only by Gonzalo, while Adrian and Francesco wait on Sebastian and Antonio. Prospero calls him "a loyal sir to him thou follow'st" in Act V, Sc. 1, 69. Gonzalo bids Adrian and Francisco to follow the conspirators in his fear of what they might attempt.

Almost his first utterance, that a man born to be hanged will not be drowned, reveals his study of human nature and his power to read human character: he thinks it better to "die a dry death" than to be drowned: no matter how badly off we are, we can be worse, Act II, Sc. 1, 1-9; there is a time to be gentle and a time to be hard, Act II, Sc. 1, 134; he would have all life governed by natural rules, not by artificiality, Act II, Sc. 1, 159-160; the manners of the supernatural are kinder than those of most human beings, Act III, Sc. 3, 30-35; and, the gods chalk out our path of life, Act V, Sc. 1, 203.

The old man grows silent only under the shock of the supernatural and the seeming impossible. He has little to say about the appearance and disappearance of the banquet, and nothing when Prospero reveals Ferdinand and Miranda at chess. At the first meeting of the court Alonso repeatedly begs him to be quiet, and Antonio and Sebastian persist in interrupting his efforts to speak about the advantages of the island and his ideal kingdom. When one subject he introduces does not win the attention of his audience he rapidly turns to another.

Summary

This honest old counsellor is kind-hearted, well-meaning, loyal, prudent, cheerful, and garrulous. He tries to make the best of a bad situation, praises the island for its air and vegetation, and finds charm in its sweet magical music.

Adrian and Francisco

These two are the only named attendants of what would be many courtiers to add dignity and display for Alonso in a ceremony so important as his daughter's marriage in a foreign court. They are both colourless and add nothing to the action of the play, each of them speaking only on two occasions. They appear to be attached to Sebastian and Antonio, as we learn in the stage direction following Act V, Sc. 1, 57.

FRANCISCO

Francisco, who seems to be the more observant, speaks only in Act II, Sc. 1 and Act III, Sc. 3. It is he who announces, in a very flowery and descriptive speech, how he saw Ferdinand buffetting the waves, and he believes that he safely reached shore. His second remark simply states that the Shapes vanished strangely.

ADRIAN

Adrian is more prosaic, unable to enter into the spirit of the raillery that attends the first meeting of the lords on the island. He falls victim to the wager between Antonio and Sebastian, but is totally unaffected by the laughter that follows. He tries to describe the island as a desert, but with a fine temperature, and the jesters will not let him complete his sentences. A little later in the same scene he shows off his knowledge of the story of Dido and Carthage, but does not seem to be sure of his geography. His only other speech contains the four closing words of Act III, Sc. 3, when he bids the unnamed lords of the court to follow him, when Gonzalo bids them keep watch over Sebastian and Antonio.

Stephano and Trinculo

Stephano and Trinculo are attendants on the court, not courtiers. Stephano is named the drunken butler, and, while he is not called upon to play any part of his calling, he is always drunk. Trinculo is the court jester, but he seldom tries to prove his wit to his title, and when he does his efforts are feeble. The two appear only by themselves and Caliban except when they are incidentally introduced at the close of the play. The dramatic purposes they serve are to reveal the natural behaviour of Caliban, to compare or contrast him with low types of humanity, and to enter into a conspiracy that will act as a foil to that of Sebastian and Antonio.

STEPHANO

He has escaped from the wreck by riding on a butt of wine to the shore, where he has hidden it among the rocks. He shaped a bottle out of the bark of a tree to keep himself supplied as he roamed over the island. He stumbled over Caliban and Trinculo lying on the ground, and from then on the three are inseparable. His masterful manner and ability to take his liquor without its showing its effects makes him supreme over the others, both of whom will do anything for him for another drink. He comes on the stage singing a ribald sailors' song, and later we find him teaching Caliban to sing. His first thought on finding Caliban is mercenary – he could make money out of the monster by showing him in Naples or selling him to some lord. In his drunken exultation he accepts the worship offered him by Caliban, considers that he is entitled to it, and declares that he will be king of the island with Trinculo and Caliban his subjects, whom he will reward with drink and punish with blows. He fears nothing but the devil, neither spirits nor men. He is delighted to possess a kingdom in which he has music for nothing. He enters into Caliban's plot to kill Prospero without any compunction whatever, especially when he learns that he can have Miranda as queen. He is purely sensual and materialistic. But, drunk as he is, he forgets the murder, and Caliban is forced over and over to keep him to it. He quarrels with Trinculo over the best robe, selects what he wants for himself, and bids Caliban to take the rest to his cave.

TRINCULO

He is the court jester, too drunk always to exhibit his wit. He tries three times to display it, but it always falls flat; he stretches out his neck like a goose and flaps his arms like a duck, Act II, Sc. 2, 23; "we steal by line and level, an't like your grace," Act IV, Sc. 1, 204; "I have been in such a pickle . . . I shall not fear fly-blowing," Act V, Sc. 1, 282. His chief characteristic is his drunkenness, so overcome after a few drinks that he is unable to stand on his feet. He quickly reveals the ugliness of his nature, his jealousy of Caliban, his insults and quarrels with him, and his subservience to Stephano. He is superstitious, afraid of thunder and of the spirits of the island. He reveals his shallowness in pointing out the ugly qualities of Caliban and mocking the superiority of his abilities over his own. Like Stephano, he too thinks of making money out of Caliban by exhibiting him.

Caliban

Caliban's dramatic importance is to serve as a contrast to Ariel, the one earthy and the other airy, to show that human beings like Stephano and Trinculo can sink lower than beasts to display the evil effects of alcohol, to plan a murder that is a burlesque to that of Antonio, and to throw light on both the goodness and sternness or severity of Prospero. When the play is put on the stage Caliban evokes more interest in his strange appearance, actions, and speeches than any other of the characters. Repulsive as he is, enjoyable elements are found in him that attract him to the audience, his appreciation of music, his poetic moments, and a natural sympathy aroused for him by his hard fate.

His mother, Sycorax, was a Moorish witch of Algiers, who, because of her too open association with the devil, was banished from her country and transported to the island of the play, together with her servant Ariel. As witches are masters of the air and can become invisible or move instantly from place to place, as shown in *Macbeth*, Shakespeare here shows how Ariel was held in subjection by Sycorax. But Ariel refused to obey some gross earthy commands of his mistress, and she imprisoned him in the cleft of a pine tree, leaving him in that condition when she died. As we learn in unexpurgated editions of the play, her consorting with him in Algiers had left her in child by him at the time of her banishment. Consequently Caliban was twelve years old when Prospero came to the island and twenty-four at the time of the play. Such parentage results in physical deformity, brutishness, lack of moral sense and a supernatural lightness or airiness of mind which is shown in his later flights of imagination.

We have never seen a picture of him or presentation on the stage that must have been in Shakespeare's mind as he imagined him. He is half fish and half man, but with human head and limbs. His trunk should be elongated and covered with scales and provided with fins. His mouth and cheeks could easily be made fish-like. Prospero calls him a tortoise, and Trinculo states that he looks and smells like a fish, a plain fish and marketable. But he is purely a land animal, living and breathing in the air, and he rejoices much in sprawling on the ground in the heat of the sun.

Many have drawn attention to the anagram or interchanging of letters in his name, making Cannibal out of Caliban. There is nothing in the play to indicate that he was cannibalistic unless we consider that his food consists of crabs, marmosets, and scammels (snails), which he promises to find for Stephano. Their low nature may be akin to his own.

When Prospero found him at the age of twelve, he had no intelligible language, no knowledge of human beings, and no morality. Prospero took him into his cell, taught him Italian, and tried to make him human in all respects. The fine language he used at times bears evidence of the kind of culture taught him. But because of his lack of morality, of a sense of decency, of a knowledge of right and wrong, he misbehaved himself and was driven from the company of Miranda and Prospero and reduced to the state of a slave. Since mental and moral punishment meant nothing to him, it became necessary to punish him physically with cramps and pains for any disobedience.

Even though he is a savage and unaccustomed to drink, he is better able to carry it than the supposedly civilized men of the court. He is less of a brute after drinking than either Trinculo or Stephano. The only effect it shows on him is to make him stammer in his song. He grows merry instead of quarrelsome like Trinculo. He is the only one of the three sober enough to see through Ariel's trick of the line of fine garments and he wants to have nothing to do with it.

His companions on the island were only the lowly animal life, the beetles, snakes, birds, and shell-fish. His thoughts cling to the earthy, the rocks, shores, trees, and sunshine on the island. He constantly talks of clouds and island noises, bogs, fens, and flats, apes, hedgehogs, and snakes. He has the intelligence of an animal, and, like a parrot or dog, can be taught to talk or do clever tricks beyond other animals. He seems to belong as much to the soil as the creeping, running things found under an upturned stone or stump of a tree.

He knows that there is a power above him, taught to him by his mother and Prospero. He fears and grows angry with the spirits which inflict pains on him. He considers wine, which he calls "water with berries in it," something divine, and when he encounters Stephano with a constant supply of it, he falls to the ground before him, calls him a god, kisses his foot, and becomes his follower. In Act I, Sc. 2, 165 he tells us that he must obey his mother's god, Setebos, which, strangely enough, is the name of the god of the Patagonian Indians in South America. Shakespeare introduced it here merely as one of the strange creatures, customs, and men brought to England by returning travellers, and surrounded by the same mystery that envelops Caliban and Sycorax.

The nature of his religion has aroused Browning to describe in one of his famous poems, Caliban on Setebos.

Prospero left him liberty to express frankly his thoughts, with the result that he becomes scurrilous in complaining of his pains and the loss of his island which he had inherited from his mother. He knows that Prospero is aware of all his actions and that it would be futile for him to try to kill him. But when he finds a god and king who is certainly divine, he craftily persuades him by the promise of giving him Miranda to murder him by some crude device which he no doubt has been long considering, and to become in reality king of the island. He is not seriously offended by Trinculo's denunciations and did not retaliate beyond urging Stephano to beat him again.

His appreciation of the sun, moon, earth, and the springs and wild creatures of the island is expressed in fine poetic and picturesque language. We find it in "As wicked dew as e'er my mother brush'd with raven's feather from unwholesome fen," and in "hedgehogs which lie tumbling in my barefoot way," and in "adders with cloven tongues hiss me in my barefoot way," and in "adders with cloven tongues hiss me into madness." He delights in the beautiful music with which the island is filled, and he urges Stephano to teach him to sing. He grows merry instead of offensive, like Trinculo, when he is drunk. He is grateful to Stephano for the liquor and promises to serve him loyally. And finally, he promises Prospero "I'll be wise hereafter and seek her grace."

Summary

Half human and half beast, he carries out a double role; revengeful and appreciative, drunk and sober, cursing and merry-making, poetic and coarse, materialistic and worshipful, obscene and attractive, shrewd and gullible.

Ariel

Ariel is a Hebrew word, meaning altar or spirit of God. Milton uses it as the name of one of the fallen angels in Paradise Lost, and Pope in Rape of the Lock as a sylph, a being at once material and immaterial, much the same as Ariel of the play. It is confused today with aerial, pertaining to the air, in which sense the author uses it in the play for the spirit of the air.

It is rather difficult for us to imagine Ariel of the play as a man instead of a woman when we think of his lightfulness and gracefulness, his yielding nature and his fairy-like qualities, but his delight in harsh work, rough-and-ready treatment of his victims, and trickery is more natural in males, as in Puck in A Midsummer Night's Dream. When artists attempt to picture him in The Tempest, they make him look feminine rather than masculine.

He was the servant of the witch Sycorax in Algiers, accompanied her to the island twenty-four years before the story, refused to obey her commands, was imprisoned by her in the cleft of a pine tree, and left in that predicament when she died. Prospero, by his knowledge of magic, released him, but forced him to serve him on pain of being imprisoned in a much harder oak tree if he disobeyed. The twelve years of servitude, probably with little to keep him employed, became vexatious, and he complains bitterly at the opening of the story, demanding to be set free. But the action proceeds so rapidly during the afternoon that he makes no further demands for freedom, buoyed up with activities and Prospero's promises.

Air extends everywhere, from the deepest mines to unknown regions above the earth, exercises its power on the sea, in fires, clouds, vegetable and animal life, takes form in the reflections of mirrors and mirages, and by its means we hear the thunder and see the lightning. The air bloweth where it listeth. Consequently Ariel is master of almost every phenomenon and his power is universal, mastering storms, wrecks, creating music, beating tabors, blowing horns, barking like dogs, summoning spirits and mortals, or producing at least mirages of banquets and glittering garments.

He takes part in the action more than a score of times. He creates the storm that wrecks the ship; he puts the passengers ashore in four different groups, each believing the others lost; he restores their clothing after ruination by sea water; he charms the crew to sleep under the hatches and puts the ship in good condition in a secret cove; he sends the fleet to which the ship belongs on to Naples; he inflicts pains on Caliban according to Prospero's orders; he leads Ferdinand to Miranda and Prospero; invisible, he plays solemn music to put the courtiers to sleep; he awakens Gonzalo with a song to prevent the murder of Alonso; invisible, he starts the quarrel between Sebastian and the others by charging them with lying; with a tabor and pipe he plays the tune which the revellers are too drunk to sing properly; he plays music as the banquet is brought in; in the form of a harpy he makes the banquet vanish to the accompaniment of thunder and lightning; he produces Ceres, Iris, Juno, and the nymphs; with his tabor he leads the drunkards through briars and thorns into a bog and deprives them of their bottle; he performs the trickery of the garments on the line; with Prospero's help he sets the dogs on the drunkards; he confines the courtiers in a grove, all distracted or mourning; he appeals to Prospero to show mercy to the repentant courtiers; he leads the courtiers into the magic ring; with a song he changes Prospero's magic robe into a courtly one; he brings the mariners to the magic ring, and finally he adds Caliban, Stephano, and Trinculo to the others.

Ariel sings only three songs himself, though he directs others. Each song exhibits a different mood, but all in anticipation of what is to develop. In the first is wonderment as he introduces Ferdinand to Prospero and Miranda, "Come unto these yellow sands." The second is premonition of evil as he puts the courtiers asleep to give Antonio and Sebastian opportunity to plot against Alonso, "While you here do snoring lie." The third is relief in his knowledge of early release as he changes Prospero's robes, "Where the bee sucks, there suck I."

Spirits are naturally unchangeable in character, but human tendencies are revealed in them in their relations with human beings. We find Ariel resentful over the loss of his freedom and the threat of the oak tree hanging over him, when he first appears to Prospero. But he grows calm as his master praises him and promises that his freedom is near. He is always eager for praise and whenever he reports what he has done, he must be told that it was done well. He is child-like in his fondness for play, freedom to run about, and mischief. His sympathy for the suffering courtiers is a quite human characteristic, not supposed to be that of a spirit, as he himself acknowledges. We are left uncertain as to whether it is his own initiative or by a command of Prospero that he gives the lie to Trinculo's remarks, or perplexes the courtiers in the linden grove, or leads the three drunken men into the bog, but in either case he finds enjoyment in his mischievous tricks, and perhaps a little malice. But everywhere he is ethereal, frolicsome, sprightly, alert, playing many of the tricks the wind does to mortals. To deserving people he is as welcome as the breezes of spring, but to the guilty he becomes tempest, thunder, and lightning.

Character Contrasts

Ariel

Spirit of air.
Soul-less being.
Speedy and dainty.
Associated with bees and
    flowers.
Desires freedom.
Serves Prospero willingly.
Raises a storm at sea
Casts spells.

Caliban

Creature of earth.
A soul in darkness.
Clumsy and uncouth.
Associated with adders
    and hedgehogs.
Desires vengeance.
Services Prospero reluctantly.
Does menial services.
Is tormented with cramps.

Antonio

Brother of Prospero.
Criminal of twelve years'
    standing.
The temptor in crime.
Without a conscience.
Decisive in action.
Tempted to crime by brother's
    neglect of duty.
Leader in mockery of Gonzalo
    and other courtiers.

Sebastian

Brother of Alonso.
Innocent of any revealed crime.
The tempted in crime.
Possessed a conscience, but
    feared it.
Slothful and hesitant in action
Tempted to crime by the
    opportunity offered to him
    by Antonio.
An echo of Antonio in
    mockery, repeating or
    commenting on the other's
    jests.

Stephano

The court butler.
Escaped from wreck by a
    butt of wine.
Able to carry his liquor.
Masterful and overbearing.
Fearless of thunder and spirits.
Presumes to be king of the island.

Trinculo

The court jester.
Escaped by swimming like
    a duck.
Incapacitated by liquor.
Quarrelsome, but submissive.
Terrified by thunder and spirits.
Content to be a subject.

Caliban

Half human, half beast.
Skilled in knowledge of nature.
Dominated by hatred of
    Prospero.
Possessed of an observant and
    poetic mind.
Instinctively religious.
Amoral, without moral sense.
Appreciative of kindness.

Stephano and Trinculo

Wholly human.
Regardless and unobservant
    of nature.
Dominated by love of drink
    and quarrelling.
Coarse in language and
    mercenary in mind.
Irreligious and superstitious.
Immoral, knowingly ready to
    do wrong.
Without any regard for others,
    self-seeking.

Literary Elements

Theme

Though published in 1623 at the beginning of the First Folio, *The Tempest,* together with *Cymbeline* and *A Winter's Tale,* belongs to the last period of Shakespeare's dramatic work. Its diction alone would place it there, but it has in common with these other plays a high moral seriousness. The period of bitter tragedy is over and the serenity of one who has risen from its dark depths casts sweetness and light over human relations. There is a strange otherworldliness about these last comedies, so different from the gay brilliance of the earlier ones, that they have been called "Romances."

The theme of our play would seem to be forgiveness – after repentance; yet Alonso's mood shortly before Prospero's revelations is rather one of mad despair induced by supernatural terrors than the true remorse of a guilty soul. Indeed, the wrong done is so far back that Alonso has to be reminded of it; and then it becomes to him just a reason for the loss that overwhelms him.

Prospero, in one sense the author of all that takes place on the stage, is rejoicing over the complete success of his "project," when the remark let slip by Ariel that his heart would melt at the sight of the sufferers, *were he human,* brings him to that merciful decision which would appear to have been his ultimate goal throughout.

In these last plays shines the radiance of womanly perfection. Miranda is not a suffering heroine like Hermione or Imogen, nor is she lost and restored (except in the sense playfully adopted by Prospero), but she shares with Marina and Perdita the ethereal beauty of unspoilt maidenhood.

Typical, too, is the avoidance of a tragic ending; not only are the criminals and the blunderers prevented from causing death – they are forgiven. All ends in peace and reconciliation, with music no mere incident as in the earlier comedies, but an active accompaniment of the action, intensifying by voice and instrument the atmosphere of enchantment.

There is another element in the play less perceptible to us, but certainly of interest to a Jacobean audience. This is what is still called the colonial problem – the landless native exploited by the white invader (who has been attracted by the fertility of newly discovered territories, but is unable to work in their climate), the forced labour and the hateful traffic in liquor.

Some critics have seen in Prospero Shakespeare's symbolic farewell to the stage. The student should try to decide this matter for himself, but he may well ask himself first, would Shakespeare really like to see himself in the severe, often ungracious character of the magician-duke? And secondly, if Naples is intended to represent Stratford-on-Avon, is it likely that the prospective occupant of New Place, whose opinion of the populace is barely concealed in his works, would, even as a gesture, seek its permission to retire? Further, it is by no means certain that *The Tempest* was the last of his plays.

Certainly, in this final period, Shakespeare shows a growing detachment from his characters. The same skill is there, but the outline is less clear, the features not so well-defined. Perhaps, with every third thought of the grave, he was more concerned with human destiny as a whole than with individual peculiarities, more intent to show that good may come of evil than that Caliban had a soul. In the composition of the dialogue and the management of plots (here *The Tempest* is an exception) are signs of that carelessness which left his literary works to the mercy of chance and the charitable endeavours of the two fellow-players whose First Folio did not appear till 1623.

However, these uncertainties and incongruities (one wonders why Prospero's magic was powerless to repeal his banishment) are not noticed in a play which appeals to an audience by its striking combination of the beautiful and the grotesque. It may have had topical value as a marriage piece or as a presentation of the native question or as a fantasia on statecraft, but its universal qualities, as in the bulk of Shakespeare's work, are for all time. Its spectators, having by their indulgence set Prospero free, may well come away feeling more tolerant, more understanding, more forgiving.

Setting

The description of Prospero's island is unusually, perhaps purposely vague. Placed somewhere off the route from Tunis to Naples, the island has the drowsy atmosphere and tropical violence of the "still-vex'd Bermoothes"; but such details as the nimble marmoset and the jay's nest, the crabs and filberts, and even the horse-pond, give it that native English touch which characterizes Shakespeare's scenery.

> It is, however, no ordinary island. There are
>> Some subtilties o' the isle, that will not let you
>> Believe things certain.

At Prospero's bidding, spirits assume various shapes, of hounds and apes, hedgehogs and adders, to afflict the unfortunate Caliban. To comfort him, however, there are soothing voices and twangling instruments,

> Sounds and sweet airs, that give delight and hurt not.

This music has a dramatic purpose. While Prospero's wand charms to a stand-still those who would approach too near, the unseen musicians waiting on him usher in the miraculous visions he conjures up, or Ariel is seen leading the way with pipe and tabor. Two of Ariel's songs are among the first half-dozen of Shakespeare's lyrics, and both are integral parts of the play: he sings to Ferdinand the imagined fate of the King, his father, and to Prospero his future state of freedom.

The poetry that informs so much of Shakespeare's plays is at its most imaginative in this imaginary island. Where else in literature is the poet's fancy more real and the real world more remote than in *The Tempest*? Yet the very freedom to create is a test of the dramatist's skill: he must not exceed the bounds of probability, even when working wonders of enchantment. The measure of Shakespeare's success is that the two creatures who differ from the rest in being, one a spirit and the other only half human, leave a stronger impression on the mind that the mere humans, Prospero excepted.

In this play the poet has, more than in any other of his works, given

> to airy nothing
> A local habitation and a name
> (*A Midsummer Night's Dream*, Act V, Sc. 1)

The student should compare Prospero's words in Act IV, Sc. 1, 148, "These our actors," with those of Oberon in that other comedy so like and yet so unlike *The Tempest* in its use of spirits and spells. In *A Midsummer Night's Dream* human quarrels are fomented for the amusement of the fairies; in our play the spirits are instrumental in redressing deep wrongs. They are, too, under the single control of a human magician who, testy and humourless as he may be, personifies that human wisdom which puts virtue before vengeance and beholds the transitoriness of this world.

> We are such stuff
> As dreams are made on, and our little life
> Is rounded with a sleep.

Shakespeare's "revels" have long since ended, and the actors of his day have "melted into air," but his island lives on in the world of the imagination with its sweet music and uncouth shapes, its love at first sight and its ultimate reconciliations.

The Element of Magic in the Play

Magic, merely a subject of curiosity to twentieth century intelligence, was a matter of importance in the sixteenth involving life and death to practitioners and victims. The burning of witches and the publication of many books on the subject, including one even by James I, bears witness to its place in public thought. Consequently the very full use of it in *The Tempest* would have a much greater effect on the audience than can be felt today. There were two different types of it, a maleficent one represented by witches and wizards, who sold their souls to the devil in popular belief and who were governed by him to work evil on victims. The other was beneficent, derived from studies in the occult and used generally for discover of new forces and investigation into laws of physics and other scientific research. Examples of both types are in the play, where they form a contrast, that of the witch Sycorax, very sketchily developed, and that of Prospero, very fully developed. Sycorax was allied with the devil, who gave her power over the air with its invisibility and swiftness of motion, but her evil work resulted in her banishment and death. Prospero invoked only his own mental astuteness to win greater powers. Before he was sufficiently learned his lack of wisdom indirectly led too to banishment, but afterwards he had full control over the air and greater prowess. He used them only for good, his own restoration to the throne, the welfare of his daughter, the repentance of Alonso, and punishment for the recalcitrant.

The attributes of magic used by Prospero are the robe, the wand, and his books on the subject. He never appears invisible himself, but he repeatedly puts on or off his magic robe, according to whether he has work to do as a magician or an ordinary man. Little mention is made of his wand; he disarms Ferdinand in Act I, Sc. 2, and will bury it "fathoms deep" when he adjures magic at the close of the play. His books are his chief power, and these he buries deeper "than did ever plummet sound." His robe represents his dominion over mortals, his wand the instrument of power, and the books his supernatural knowledge.

The spirits summoned by Ariel may be classified as those of fire, air, earth, and water. Fire is evoked in lightning and the forms taken by Ariel in flames on the masts and rigging of the ship, and the will-o-the-wisps used to torment Caliban. Water spirits appear in the Naiads and elves of the brooks and streams who are in attendance in the masque of Act IV to "bestow upon the eyes of this young couple some vanity of mine art," said by Prospero to Ariel, Act IV Sc. 1, 23. The spirits of air are of the highest type and include Ariel and the divinities he summons, Ceres, Iris, Juno, and the nymphs. The thunder, music, noises, sounds, and sweet airs with which the island abounds, says Caliban, pertain also to the air. The spirits of earth are the goblins, the dogs and hounds used to plague Caliban and his associates.

Another type of the magic used by Prospero, either by himself or with the aid of Ariel, is in materialistic performances, more spectacular than most of the others, such as the production and disappearance of the banquet, the line of glittering garments, the arrival and dance of the Reapers, and the magic circle in which the courtiers were held charmed.

Masque and Antimasque

The masque is the form of drama midway between a regular play and a pageant, combining the characters and action of a story with the elaborateness and display of a public celebration. It is characterized by the use of mythological personages, unusual scenery and apparel, and bright dialogues, songs, and music. The scene is laid in some ideal of unusual place, as in *The Tempest*, the supernatural occupies a large part, and the roles may be acted by amateur courtiers.

Masques were written mostly for special occasions, such as court celebrations. In wedding ceremonies entertainments were frequently conducted for a week, with a different program for each day. *The Tempest* was written expressly as one of the features of the marriage of Elizabeth, daughter of James I, and Prince Frederick, the Palatine Elector of the Holy Roman Empire, in 1611. The ideal bride and groom of the play and the blessings of the goddesses bestowed on them may be said to be the wishes of the author for the happiness of Elizabeth and Frederick.

Two so-called antimasques occur in the play to honour the wedding of Miranda and Ferdinand, just as the masque of the play honours the others. The first antimasque is the banquet scene of Act III, a dumb show with music, gestures, and dancing with the supernatural appearance and disappearance of the banquet. The second is much more elaborate and direct, appearing when Prospero summons the goddesses to entertain Ferdinand and Miranda in Act IV. Here we have mythological participants, stately measured verse, surprise after surprise from Juno down to Reapers, music, song, and ceremonious and grotesque dancing, until Prospero suddenly puts an end to it.

Usually in masques the actors present a wide variety of love stories as in *A Midsummer Night's Dream* and in *As You Like It*. But *The Tempest* is limited to a single story, making it more dignified than the others. The native simplicity of Miranda and Ferdinand must not be marred by contrasting artificialities.

Soliloquies

GENERAL PURPOSES   The purposes of soliloquies are, 1, to reveal the speaker's true character and motives; 2, to reveal his intentions; 3, to prepare the audience for subsequent developments; 4, to explain matters that happen between scenes and thereby to shorten the play by something necessary but unimportant, details that might detract from the progress of the action if made into a full scene.

The story in *The Tempest* is so compact and rapid in development that the above purposes do not always apply. Besides, soliloquies are comparatively few in number. That they are sometimes spoken in the presence of spirits is of little more consequence than that all are spoken in the presence of the speaker's mind.

PROSPERO'S THREE SOLILOQUIES   1. At the close of Act III, Sc. 1, he keeps the audience informed of his purpose to bring Ferdinand and Miranda together and he states his satisfaction in its successful accomplishment. 2. In Act IV, Sc. 1, 156, he curses Caliban after Ariel's exposure of the conspiracy of the three villians to kill him. 3. His most important soliloquy is that of Act V, in which he reviews his past magic and announces his decision to abjure it. This is intended to sum up his work for the audience and to prepare for his discarding his magic.

GONZALO speaks his only soliloquy at the close of the opening scene, in which he indicates his philosophy of life when he believes himself at the point of death. His belief is that life is sweet, but we cannot work against the will of the gods.

71

FERDINAND's single soliloquy is at the opening of Act III, just before Miranda comes to see him at work. He declaims against the menial task set for him by Prospero, but he submits to it out of love for Miranda. Its purpose is to prepare for the meeting of the two lovers and to reveal the courtliness of his character.

CALIBAN opens Act II, Sc. 3, revealing his revengeful nature in his cursing of Prospero and his spirits for the work and pains they put on him. This revelation made when he expresses his own thoughts and feelings adds very little to what Prospero told him to his face in Act I, Sc. 2.

Asides

GENERAL PURPOSES Asides are comments supposedly made for the audience alone, occurring usually in or between speeches, They are usually short, for otherwise they interrupt the couse of the play. Their usual purposes, are 1, to indicate the character of the speaker; 2, to draw the attention of the audience to the significance of what has been said; 3, to explain developments; 4, to create humour by introducing the unexpected. In this play they are made by Prospero, Ariel, Caliban, and Antonio.

PROSPERO'S first merely expresses surprise at Ferdinand's announcement of the death of the Duke of Milan and his son, the significance of which is not very clear. But the rightful Duke of Milan is himself, and he has no son, nor has the usurper, so far as later information in the play is concerned. In Act III, Sc. 1, his asides expressed delight over the success of his bringing his daughter and Ferdinand together, at the same time showing the audience that his anger with Ferdinand is only assumed. In Act III, Sc. 3, his praise of Ariel's work in the banquet helps to keep the latter in mind, and he breaks off the Reapers' dance on recalling the conspiracy of Caliban. In Act V, Sc. 1, 80, he again informs the audience of the success of the magic ring in astounding the courtiers. In line 126 of the same scene he stuns Antonio and Sebastian with exposing their plot; it is the most important of his asides, as he reveals that their future freedom from their just deserts rests only on their good behaviour.

ARIEL, in three asides, announces that he will keep Prospero informed on the plots of the criminals, or to congratulate himself on the success of his work.

CALIBAN, in Act II, Sc. 2, 112, explains his finding a god in Stephano and suggests the beginning of the plot against Prospero.

ANTONIO, Act III, Sc. 3, speaks in an aside with Sebastian to demand renewal of their plot against Alonso.

Use of Prose

The normal form of Shakespeare's plays is blank verse. When prose is used, it is for a definite purpose.

Prose is invariably used for
1. Comic characters (e.g. Stephano and Trinculo) and
2. Characters of lower social position.

This was a literary convention at a time when literature was aristocratic and the chief characters in plays (as in life) were kings and nobles. Scenes in which the lowest orders of society figure are a contrast; these people live on a lower plane of feeling than the main characters, and thereby emphasize the heights of the feeling of the main characters, and the contrast in the medium of expression – prose instead of verse – is in perfect keeping.

In this play prose and verse are frequently intermingled; such frequent transitions from one to the other mean either that the freer rhythm of Shakespeare's blank verse had by now approximated so closely to that of normal speech that it was a matter of indifference to him which he employed, or that subtle changes of tone or inflection are intended, or perhaps a combination of both.

Prospero, Ariel, Miranda and Ferdinand (serious characters) speak no prose, Stephano and Trinculo (comic characters) no verse. The others vary in ways that are worth notice. The mocking commentary of Antonio and Sebastian is in prose, the conspiracy in verse. The Boatswain on deck in the storm speaks like a real sailor; he is a different man when, at the end of the play, he narrates the marvellous adventures of the crew. When Gonzalo wishes to be witty, he chatters away in prose; when he consoles or philosophizes or rejoices, he does it in equally garrulous verse. After one brief remark on the ship prior to the loss of his son, Alonso keeps to verse for the utterance of his grief or amazement. But the most remarkable case is Caliban. Not only is this "savage and deformed slave" (according to the *dramatis personae*) by his very use of verse raised above the level of his companions, but he slips easily from one into the other. He even achieves the unique feat of saying the same thing in both: "a sorcerer, that by his cunning hath cheated me of the island" is repeated a few lines farther on in verse form, in response to Stephano's solemn "Proceed,"

I say, by sorcery he got this isle.

As a rule, the change from prose to verse marks a change to a higher pitch of feeling, be it the urgency of Antonio, the piety of Gonzalo, the amazement of the Boatswain, or the longings and maledictions of Caliban. The few puns, so prevalent in Shakespeare's earlier work, are cracked in the prose passages.

Metre

The masque, in which the dialogue is conventional and artificial, is written in "heroic couplets." The stanzas of the more attractive song by Juno and Ceres are trochaic octosyllabic quatrains. Ariel's one-stanza songs are by comparison gems of melody; respectively a dance, a lament, a warning and a paean of joy, they differ structurally, but are all trochaic.

The Serenity of *The Tempest*

Over the beauty of youth and the love of youth, there is shed, in these plays of Shakspere's final period, a clear yet tender luminousness, not elsewhere to be perceived in his writings. In his earlier plays, Shakspere writes concerning young men and maidens, their loves, their mirth, their griefs, as one who is among them, who has a lively, personal interest in their concerns, who can make merry with them, treat them familiarly, and, if need be, can mock them into good sense. There is nothing in these early plays wonderful, strangely beautiful, pathetic about youth and its joys and sorrows. In the histories and tragedies, as was to be expected, more massive, broader, or more profound objects of interest engaged the poet's imagination. But in these latest plays, the beautiful pathetic light is always present. There are the sufferers, aged, experienced, tried – Queen Katharine, Prospero, Hermione. And over against these there are the children absorbed in their happy and exquisite egoism, – Perdita and Miranda, Florizel and Ferdinand, and the boys of old Belarius.

The same means to secure ideality for these figures, so young and beautiful, is in each case (instinctively perhaps rather than deliberately) resorted to. They are lost children, – princes or a princess, removed from the court, and its conventional surroundings, into some scene of rare, natural beauty. There are the lost princes – Arviragus and Guiderius, among the mountains of Wales, drinking the free air, and offering their salutations to the risen sun. There is Perdita, the shepherdess-princess, 'queen of curds and cream', sharing with old and young her flowers, lovelier and more undying than those that Proserpina let fall from Dis's waggon. There is Miranda, (whose very name is significant of wonder), made up of beauty, and love, and womanly pity, neither courtly nor rustic, with the breeding of an island of enchantment, where Prospero is her tutor and protector, and Caliban her servant, and the Prince of Naples her lover. In each of these plays we can see Shakspere, as it were, tenderly bending over the joys and sorrows of youth. We recognise this rather through the total characterization, and through a feeling and a presence, than through definite incident or statement. But some of this feeling escapes in the disinterested joy and admiration of old Belarius when he gazes at the princely youths, and in Camillo's loyalty to Florizel and Perdita; while it obtains more distinct expression in such a word as that which Prospero utters, when from a distance he watches with pleasure Miranda's zeal to relieve Ferdinand from his task of log-bearing: – 'Poor worm, thou art infected'.[1]

It is not chiefly because Prospero is a great enchanter, now about to break his magic staff, to drown his book deeper than ever plummet sounded, to dismiss his airy spirits, and to return to the practical service of his Dukedom, that we identify Prospero in some measure with Shakspere himself. It is rather because the temper of Prospero, the grave harmony of his character, his self-mastery, his calm validity of will, his sensitiveness to wrong, his unfaltering justice, and with these, a certain abandonment, a remoteness from the common joys and sorrows of the world, are characteristic of Shakspere as discovered to us in all his latest plays. Prospero is a harmonious and fully developed *will*. In the earlier play of fairy enchantments, *A Midsummer Night's Dream,* the 'human mortals' wander to and fro in a maze of error, misled by the mischievous frolic of Puck, the jester and clown of Fairyland. But here the spirits of the elements, and Caliban the gross genius of brute-matter, – needful for the service of life, – are brought under subjection to the human will of Prospero.

What is more, Prospero has entered into complete possession of himself. Shakspere has shown us his quick sense of injury, his intellectual impatience, his occasional moment of keen irritability, in order that we may be more deeply aware of his abiding strength and self-possession, and that we may perceive how these have been grafted upon a temperament, not impassive or unexcitable. And Prospero has reached not only the higher levels of moral attainment; he has also reached an altitude of thought from which he can survey the whole of human life, and see how small and yet how great it is. His heart is sensitive, he is profoundly touched by the joy of the children, with whom in the egoism of their love he passes for a thing of secondary interest; he is deeply moved by the perfidy of his brother. His brain is readily set a-work, and can with difficulty be checked from eager and excessive energizing; he is subject to the access of sudden and agitating thought. But Prospero masters his own sensitiveness, emotional and intellectual: –

> We are such stuff
> As dreams are made on, and our little life
> Is rounded with a sleep. Sir, I am vexed;
> Bear with my weakness; my old brain is troubled:
> Be not disturb'd with my infirmity;
> If you be pleased, retire into my cell
> And there repose; a turn or two I'll walk,
> To still my beating mind.

'Such stuff as dreams are made on.' Nevertheless, in this little life, in this dream, Prospero will maintain his dream rights and fulfil his dream duties. In the dream, he, a Duke, will accomplish Duke's work. Having idealized everything, Shakspere left everything real. Bishop Berkeley's foot was no less able to set a pebble flying than was the lumbering foot of Dr. Johnson. Nevertheless, no material substance intervened between the soul of Berkeley and the immediate presence of the play of Divine power.

A thought which seems to run through the whole of *The Tempest*, appearing here and there like a coloured thread in some web, is the thought that the true freedom of man consists in service. Ariel, untouched by human feeling, is panting for his liberty; in the last words of Prospero are promised his enfranchisement and dismissal to the elements. Ariel reverences his great master, and serves him with bright alacrity; but he is bound by none of our human ties, strong and tender, and he will rejoice when Prospero is to him as though he never were.[2] To Caliban, a land-fish, with the duller elements of earth and water in his composition, but no portion of the higher elements, air and fire, though he receives dim intimations of a higher world, – a musical humming, or a twangling, or a voice heard in sleep – to Caliban, service is slavery.[3] He hates to bear his logs; he fears the incomprehensible power of Prospero, and obeys, and curses. The great master has usurped the rights of the brute-power Caliban. And when Stephano and Trinculo appear, ridiculously impoverished specimens of humanity, with their shallow understandings and vulgar greeds, this poor earth-monster is possessed by a sudden *schwärmerei*, a fanaticism for liberty! –

> 'Ban, 'ban, Ca'-Caliban,
> Has a new master; get a new man.
> Freedom, heyday! heyday, freedom! freedom! freedom,
> heyday, freedom!

His new master also sings his impassioned hymn of liberty, the *Marseillaise* of the enchanted island:

> Flout 'em and scout 'em,
> And scout 'em and flout 'em;
> Thought is free.

The leaders of the revolution, escaped from the stench and foulness of the horse-pond, King Stephano and his prime minister Trinculo, like too many leaders of the people, bring to an end their great achievement on behalf of liberty by quarrelling over booty, – the trumpery which the providence of Prospero had placed in their way. Caliban, though scarce more truly wise or instructed than before, at least discovers his particular error of the day and hour:

> What a thrice-double ass
> Was I, to take this drunkard for a god,
> And worship this dull fool!

It must be admitted that Shakspere, if not, as Hartley Coleridge asserted, 'a Tory and a gentleman', had within him some of the elements of English conservatism.

But while Ariel and Caliban, each in his own way, is impatient of service, the human actors, in whom we are chiefly interested, are entering into bonds – bonds of affection, bonds of duty, in which they find their truest freedom. Ferdinand and Miranda emulously contend in the task of bearing the burden which Prospero has imposed upon the prince:

> I am in my condition
> A prince, Miranda; I do think, a king:
> I would, not so! and would no more endure
> This wooden slavery than to suffer
> The flesh-fly blow my mouth. Hear my soul speak:
> The very instant that I saw you, did
> My heart fly to your service; there resides,
> To make me slave to it; and for your sake
> Am I this patient log-man.

And Miranda speaks with the sacred candour from which spring the nobler manners of a world more real and glad than the world of convention and proprieties and pruderies:

> Hence, bashful cunning!
> And prompt me, plain and holy innocence!
> I am your wife, if you will marry me;
> If not, I'll die your maid: to be your fellow
> You may deny me; but I'll be your servant
> Whether you will or no.
> *Fer.* My mistress, dearest;
> And I thus humble ever.
> *Mir.* My husband, then?
> *Fer.* Ay, with a heart as willing
> As bondage e'er of freedom.

In an earlier part of the play, this chord which runs through it had been playfully struck in the description of Gonzalo's imaginary commonwealth, in which man is to be enfranchised from all the laborious necessities of life. Here is the ideal of notional liberty, Shakspere would say, and to attempt to realise it at once lands us in absurdities and self-contradictions:

> For no kind of traffic
> Would I admit: no name of magistrate;
> Letters should not be known: riches, poverty,
> And use of service none; contract, succession,
> Bourn, bound of land, tilth, vineyard, none;
> No use of metal, corn, or wine, or oil;
> No occupation; all men idle, all,
> And women too, but innocent and pure;
> No sovereignty.
> *Seb.* Yet he would be king on't.[4]

Finally, in the Epilogue, which was written perhaps by Shakspere, perhaps by some one acquainted with his thoughts, Prospero in his character of a man, no longer a potent enchanter, petitions the spectators of the theatre for two things, pardon and freedom. It would be straining matters to discover in this Epilogue profound significances. And yet in its playfulness it curiously falls in with the moral purport of the whole. Prospero, the pardoner, implores pardon. Shakspere was aware – whether such be the significance (aside - - for the writer's mind) of this Epilogue or not – that no life is ever lived which does not need to receive as well as to render forgiveness. He knew that every energetic dealer with the world must seek a sincere and liberal pardon for many things. Forgiveness and freedom: these are keynotes of the play. When it was occupying the mind of Shakspere, he was passing from his service as artist to his service as English country gentleman. Had his mind been dwelling on the question of how he should employ his new freedom, and had he been enforcing upon himself the truth that the highest freedom lies in the bonds of duty?[5]

By Edward Dowden

Notes

[1]The same feeling appears in the lines which end Act III, Scene 1.
Prospero. So glad of this as they cannot be,
Who are surprised with all; but my rejoicing
At nothing can be more.
[2]Ariel is promised his freedom after two days, Act I, Scene 2. Why two days? The time of the entire action of the Tempest is only three hours. What was to be the employment of Ariel during two days? To make the winds and seas favourable during the voyage to Naples. Prospero's island therefore was imagined by Shakspere as within two days' quick sail of Naples.
[3]The conception of Caliban, the 'servant-monster', 'plain fish and no doubt marketable', the 'tortoise', 'his fins like arms', with 'a very ancient and fish-like smell', who gabbled until Prospero taught him language – this conception was in Shakspere's mind when he wrote *Troilus and Cressida*. Thersites describes Ajax (Act III, Sc. 3): '*He's grown a very land-fish, languageless, a monster.*'
[4]Act II, Scene 1. – The prolonged and dull joking of Sebastian in this scene cannot be meant by Shakespeare to be really bright and witty. It is meant to shew that the intellectual poverty of the conspirators is as great as their moral obliquity. They are monsters more ignoble than Caliban. Their laughter is 'the crackling of thorns under a pot'.
[5]Mr Furnivall, observing that in these later plays breaches of the family bond are dramatically studied, and the reconciliations are domestic reconciliations in *Cymbeline* and *The Winter's Tale*, suggests to me that they were a kind of confession on Shakspere's part that he had inadequately felt the beauty and tenderness of the common relations of father and child, wife and husband; and that he was now quietly resolving to be gentle, and wholly just to his wife and his home. I cannot altogether make this view of the later plays my own, and leave it to the reader to accept and develop as he may be able.

The Mirror of Analogy

The Mind, that Ocean where each kind
Does streight its own resemblance find;
Yet it creates, transcending these,
Far other Worlds, and other Seas . . .

Andrew Marvell

Of *The Tempest*, we may say what Ferdinand said of the masque,

> This is a most majestic vision, and
> Harmonious charmingly.

The harmony of the play lies in its metaphorical design, in the closeness and completeness with which its rich and varied elements are linked through almost inexhaustible analogies. It is hard to pick a speech at random without coming on an expression that brings us by analogy into direct contact with elements that seem remote because of their place in the action or because of the type of experience they symbolize. Opening the play at the second act we read,

> Four legs and two voices; a most delicate monster!

The last phrase is comic enough as used of Caliban and as issuing from the lips of Stephano, a 'most foul' speaker. But 'delicate' evokes a more subtle incongruity by recalling characters and a world we might suppose were forgotten. Stephano is parodying Prospero when he rebukes Ariel as 'a spirit too delicate / To act her [Sycorax's] earthy and abhorr'd commands' and when he says,

> delicate Ariel,
> I'll set thee free for this!

We have in Stephano's words not only the familiar Shakespearean balancing of comic and serious, but a counterpointing of analogies that run throughout the play. 'Delicate' as the anti-thesis of 'earth' points to the opposition of Ariel and Caliban and to the often recurring earth-air symbolism of *The Tempest*. 'Delicate' used of this remarkable island creature echoes also the 'delicate temperance' of which the courtiers spoke and 'the air' that 'breathes . . . here most sweetly'. 'Monster' – almost another name for Caliban – balances these airy suggestions with an allusion to 'the people of the island . . . of monstrous shape' and thereby to the strain of fantastic sea lore in *The Tempest*, which is being parodied in this scene.

So viewed, Shakespeare's analogies may perhaps seem too much like exploding nebulae in an expanding though hardly ordered universe. But Shakespeare does not 'multiply variety in a wilderness of mirrors'; he makes use of a few fairly constant analogies that can be traced through expressions sometimes the same and sometimes extraordinarily varied. And the recurrent analogies (or continuities) are linked through a key metaphor into a single metaphorical design. Shakespeare is continually prodding us – often in ways of which we are barely conscious – to relate the passing dialogue with other dialogues into and through a super-design of metaphor.

In concentrating on how the design is built up, I am not forgetting that it is a metaphorical design in a *drama,* that we are interested in how Shakespeare has linked stages in a presentation of changing human relationships. Toward the end of the chapter I hope to show how wonderfully the metaphorical design is related to the main dramatic sequence of *The Tempest*, especially in the climactic speeches of Acts IV and V.

The play moves forward, we should remember, from a scene of tempest to a final promise of 'calm seas, auspicious gales', and through a series of punishments or trials to a series of reconciliations and restorations. Although, as Dr. Johnson might say, there is a 'concatenation of events' running through Prospero's 'project' and though the play has a curiously exact time schedule, there is often little chronological or logical connection between successive dialogues or bits of action. To be sure, Shakespeare has the Elizabethan conventions on his side, but the freedom of his dramatic composition in *The Tempest* never seems merely conventional or capricious because the linkage of analogy is so varied and so pervasive.

The surest proof of the pervasiveness of Shakespeare's design lies in the mere number of continuities that can be discovered in the play. But some are more important than others because they can be traced through more expressions or in more scenes and because they express analogies more closely related to the key metaphor. The six main continuities, roughly labeled to indicate their character, are: 'strange-wondrous', 'sleep-and-dream', 'sea-tempest', 'music-and-noise', 'earth-air', 'slavery-freedom', and 'sovereignty-conspiracy'.

All of these continuities appear during the second scene of Act I, which is an exposition of Shakespeare's metaphorical and dramatic designs for the entire play. Near the close of the scene, Ariel's two songs offer wonderfully concentrated expressions of both designs. 'Come unto these yellow sands' calms the 'fury' of the waves and Ferdinand's 'passion', thus charting in brief the course of the action. 'Full fathom five' is anticipatory in a very different fashion. It presents in miniature the main lines of the metaphorical design and sounds the key note of 'sea change', Shakespeare's most direct expression of the key metaphor of *The Tempest*. (Act I, Sc. 2, I-186.)

As we trace the first two continuities ('strange-wondrous', 'sleep-and-dream'), the reader can appreciate how unobtrusively they emerge from the developing dramatic pattern. Prospero's narrative, with which the scene opens, tells us of the past and describes the present situation while symbolizing the quality of *The Tempest* world. Prospero explains that his enemies have come to this shore 'by accident most strange', and Miranda, who falls to sleep at the end of his tale, accounts for her lapse by saying,

> The strangeness of your story put
> Heaviness in me.

Prospero's tale was strange indeed: it included a ruler 'rapt in secret studies', a 'false uncle' who 'new created / The creatures' of the state, the miraculous voyage of Prospero and Miranda (who was 'a cherubin') and their safe arrival 'by Providence divine'. This 'strangeness' is best defined by Alonso's remarks near the end of the play:

These are not natural events; they strengthen
From strange to stranger . . .

This is as strange a maze as e'er men trod;
And there is in this business more than nature
Was ever conduct of . . .

They are 'unnatural' in a broad seventeenth-century sense of the term; that is, outside the order which includes all created things. The theme is almost constantly being played on: 'strange', 'strangely', or 'strangeness' occur altogether some seventeen times, and similar meanings are echoed in 'wondrous', 'monstrous', 'divine'.

Of all the analogies of the play this is probably the vaguest, the nearest in effect to the atmospheric unity of nineteenth-century Romantic poetry. But a more precise metaphor of strangeness appears, the 'strangeness' of 'new created creatures'. From the 'accident most strange' of the shipwreck we come to Alonso's ponderous woe:

O thou, mine heir
Of Naples and of Milan! what strange fish
Hath made his meal on thee?

and then to Trinculo's discovery of Caliban – 'A strange fish!' With a similar comic antiphony, Miranda finds Ferdinand 'a thing divine', and Ferdinand replies, 'O you wonder'; while a little later hails Trinculo as his god and cries, 'Thou wondrous man'. The full significance of these strange births will appear later.

The vague 'strangeness' of the island world is closely allied to a state of sleep, both continuities appearing in Miranda's remark about the 'heaviness' that came over her while listening to Prospero's story. The feeling that we are entering on an experience of sleep-and-dream arises beautifully out of the dramatic and rhythmic texture of the opening dialogue between father and daughter. The movement of these speeches with their oddly rocking repetitions is in key with the sleepy incredibility of the events about to be described: 'Canst thou remember . . . thou canst . . . I can . . . thy remembrance . . . my remembrance . . . thou remember'st . . . Twelve year since, Miranda, twelve year since . . .' Throughout the story Prospero is continually reminding Miranda to 'attend' to the telling, and it seems perfectly natural that at the end she should be 'inclin'd to sleep'. (Note in passing how neatly Shakespeare has broken a long narrative into dialogue and also given a distinct impression of Prospero's firmness and of Miranda's innocent dependence.) Miranda's images of the past come back to her 'rather like a dream', and Prospero seems to be drawing their story from a world of sleep, 'the dark backward and abysm of time'.

With the next scene (the mourning King and his courtiers) we meet one of Shakespeare's typical analogical progressions. The sleep which affects the courtiers is, like Miranda's, a strange 'heaviness'. Their dialogue runs down, psychologically and rhythmically, through three echoes of Miranda's words:

> *Gonzalo.* Will you laugh me asleep, for I am very heavy? . . .
> *Sebastian.* Do not omit the heavy offer of it . . .
> *Alonso.* Thank you. Wondrous heavy.
> *Sebastian.* What a strange drowsiness possesses them!

The conversation that follows between the conspirators shows how Shakespeare uses an analogy to move to a new level of action and experience and to make them harmonious with what precedes and follows. Sebastian and Antonio begin by talking about actual sleep and waking: why are they not drowsy like the others? Then Antonio shifts to talking of sleepiness and alertness of mind, and from that to imagining that he sees 'a crown dropping' upon Sebastian's head. The wit becomes more complex as Sebastian describes Antonio's talk as 'sleepy language' – without meaning – though indicating that it does have meaning. 'There's meaning in thy snores.' This dialogue, which readers are liable to dismiss as so much Elizabethan wit, has its place within the play's metaphorical pattern. The plotting takes on a preposterous dreamy-sleepy character like that of Prospero's narrative and Miranda's recollections. Through such verbal trifling Shakespeare maintains the continuous quality of his imagined world.

References to similar wakings and sleepings, to dreams and dreamlike states, abound from here to the end of the play, where the sailors are 'brought moping . . . even in a dream', and the grand awakening of all the characters is completed. But up to that point confusion between waking and sleep is the rule, being awake is never far from sleep or dream. In *The Tempest* sleep is always imminent, and more than once action ends in sleep or trance.

The witty talk of the conspirators glides from conceits of 'sleep' to conceits of 'the sea', to talk of 'standing water' and 'flowing' and 'ebbing'. The 'good Gonzalo', in consoling the King, speaks in similar figures:

> It is foul weather in us all, good sir,
> When you are cloudy.

Recurrent expressions of 'sea and tempest', like those of 'sleep and dream', are numerous and have a similar atmospheric value of not letting us forget the special quality of life on Prospero's island. But they also have far more important effects, for many of them become metaphors which are more precisely and more variously symbolic and which link more kinds of experience together.

By tracing two groups of 'tempest' expressions, metaphors of 'sea-swallowing' and images of 'clouds', we may understand how these more complex analogies are built up. We may also see how Shakespeare moves from narrative fact to metaphor, from image or metaphor referring only to narrative fact to metaphor rich in moral and psychological implications. As in creating the analogies of 'strangeness' and 'sleep', Shakespeare starts from a dramatic necessity: the audience must be told what the situation was in the storm scene with which the play opens, and they must learn through an actor (Miranda) how they are to take it. (See Act I, Sc. 2, I-186.) Although there is a hint of magic in Miranda's vision of the tempest, she pictures it as a violent actuality:

> Had I been any god of power, I would
> Have sunk the sea within the earth, or e'er
> It should the good ship so have swallow'd and
> The fraughting souls within her.

As if there were an inner rhythm in these responses, this metaphor, like others we have been tracing, recurs in the plotting episode. Antonio is speaking of his sister Claribel, left behind in Tunis:

> she that from whom
> We all were sea-swallow'd, though some cast again,
> And by that destiny to perform an act
> Whereof what's past is prologue, what to come
> In yours and my discharge.

In this new context 'sea-swallow'd' does several things at once. It brings back Miranda's horrified impression; but the magical nature of the storm now being known, the phrase reminds us that there was no 'sea-swallowing', no actual sinking of 'fraughting souls'. Next, with a curiously Shakespearean 'glide and a jump' via the pun on 'cast', 'sea-swallow'd' merges into another metaphor (they are now 'cast' as actors in destiny's drama). 'Sea-swallowing' has become a metaphor that expresses destiny's extraordinary way of bringing Sebastian to the throne.

The irony of Antonio's words, which is clear to the audience, is made explicit later in the solemn speech in which Ariel explains the purpose of the tempest:

> You are three men of sin, whom Desty –
> That hath no instrument this lower world
> And what is in 't – the never-surfeited sea
> Hath caused to belch up you . . .

Few passages could show better how Shakespeare carries his analogies along and at the same time completely renews them. The 'belching up' recalls the wreck and the casting ashore and the earlier connection with destiny. But the sea's action is now described in much grosser terms and with grim sarcasm, while the oddly compact grammar makes 'the never-surfeited sea' very nearly a synonym for 'Destiny'. The violence though increased is now religous and moral; the imagery has become expressive of the strenuous punishment and purification of 'three men of sin'. So by the continuity of his varying metaphor Shakespeare has expressed an unbroken transition from actual storm to the storm of the soul. This sequence, which expresses both physical and metaphysical transformations, points very clearly to the key metaphor of *The Tempest*.

The recurrent cloud images present a similar sequence as they take on various symbolic meanings in the course of the play. 'Cloud' does not actually occur in the opening storm scene, but when Trinculo sees 'another storm brewing' and speaks of a 'black cloud', we are reminded of the original tempest. The cloud undergoes an appropriate change in Trinculo's speech; it 'looks like a foul bombard that would shed his liquor'. This comic cloud is very different from 'the curl'd clouds' on which Ariel rides, though they too are associated with storms. The clouds of Caliban's exquisite speech are those of Ariel and the deities of the masque:

> and then, in dreaming,
> The clouds methought would open and show riches
> Ready to drop upon me . . .

Clouds – here linked with magical riches – become in Prospero's 'cloud-capp'd towers' speech a symbol for the unsubstantial splendor of the world. One of the subordinate metaphors there, the 'melting into air' and the 'dissolving' of the clouds, is picked up in Prospero's later words about the courtiers:

> The charm dissolves apace;
> And as the morning steals upon the night,
> Melting the darkness, so their rising senses
> Begin to chase the ignorant fumes that mantle
> Their clearer reason.

This dissolution of night clouds (suggested also by 'fumes') is a figure for the change from madness to sanity, from evil ignorance to the clear perceptions of reason. Although the cloud images of the play are so varied, they have a common symbolic value, for whether they are clouds of tempest or of visionary riches or of the soul, they are always magically unsubstantial. The reader is led to feel some touch of likeness among experiences as different as a storm at sea, a bit of drunken whimsy, a vision of heavenly and earthly beauty, and a spiritual regeneration. The cloud sequence, as an arc of metaphor, is in perfect relation to the gradual dramatic movement from the tempest and punishment to fair weather and reconciliation, the images having meanings more and more remote from any actual storm.

The 'cloudlike' change in the distracted souls of the guilty nobles was induced (as if in reminiscence of Plato) by *Solemn music* –

> A solemn air and the best comforter
> To an unsettled fancy.

Many of the expressions referring to music, like the stage direction above, are not explicitly metaphorical, but along with the continuities of 'sleep' and 'strangeness' they help maintain the magical character of the action. The music is always the music of spirits and always a sign of more than natural events.

The one fairly constant musical metaphor[1] in *The Tempest* is the symbolic opposition of confused noises, especially storm sounds, and harmonious music. The key word and the central impression of the opening scene is certainly 'noise'[2] in the modern sense. The impression is carried over in the first words of the next scene:

> If by your art, my dearest father, you have
> Put the wild waters in this roar, allay them.

Miranda's request is soon answered by Ariel's first song, 'the wild waves' are 'whist'. The *solemn and strange music* heard when the *strange Shapes* bring a banquet to the courtiers makes Alonso say, 'What harmony is this? my good friends, hark!' Gonzalo replies: 'Marvelous sweet music!' By contrast, when Ariel enters shortly after, in order to inform the 'three men of sin' of their punishment by the storm, there is an offstage sound of *Thunder and Lightning*. The masque vision which Ferdinand finds 'harmonious charmingly' is rudely interrupted by *a strange, hollow, and confused noise* which symbolizes the stormy anger expressed by Prospero in the speeches that follow. When in the next scene he prepares to forgive his enemies, he abjures the 'rough magic' by which he

> call'd forth the mutinous winds,
> And 'twixt the green sea and the azur'd vault
> Set roaring war . . .

As the *solemn music* is played the clouds of ignorance 'dissolve', and so the musical metaphor, like the sea metaphor, has moved from outer to inner weather.

The music analogy has some close links with the earth-air continuity which we glanced at in the introductory chapter of the book. Ferdinand, following Ariel's 'yellow sands' song, asks, 'Where should this music be? i' th' air, or th' earth?' And a little later:

85

This is no mortal business, nor no sound
That the earth owes: I hear it now above me.

The connection of air and music can never be long forgotten: Ariel and his spirits of 'thin air' are the musicians of the island.

The earth-air, Caliban-Ariel antithesis coincides at points with what we might call a slavery-freedom continuity, for Caliban is in Prospero's words both 'slave' and 'earth'. Ariel too is called a 'slave' by Prospero, and for the time of the play he is as much a slave as Caliban. (Both are called 'slaves' in I ii, the scene of metaphorical exposition.) He is always asking for his freedom, which is at last granted, his release being symbolically expressed in the airy rovings of his final song. He flies into perpetual summer and, like air, becomes merged with the elements. By contrast, the 'high-day, freedom!' of which Caliban sings is ironically enough simply a change of masters.

The 'slaves' and 'servants' of the play suffer various kinds of imprisonment, from Ariel in his 'cloven pine' to Ferdinand's mild confinement, and before the end of Act IV everyone except Prospero and Miranda has been imprisoned in one way or another. During the course of Act V all the prisoners except Ferdinand (who has already been released) are set free, each of them by Prospero's special command.

A sovereignty-conspiracy analogy parallels very closely the slavery-freedom analogy, some of the same persons, e.g. Ferdinand and Caliban, appearing as both slaves and conspirators. 'That foul conspiracy / Of the beast Caliban, and his confederates' is of course a parody version of the 'Open-ey'd Conspiracy' of Sebastian and Antonio. Ferdinand, too, is charged fantastically by Prospero with plotting against his island rule. Talk of kings and royalty turns up in many scenes, being connected usually with the denial of kingship, as in 'good Gonzalo's' speech on his golden-age commonwealth where 'he would be king' and yet have 'no sovereignty'. Though no single explicit metaphor for conspiracy or usurpation is often repeated, Shakespeare rings many changes on the theme as he moves from plot to plot. Prospero's brother, we recall, is said to have 'new created the creatures' of state. Alonso's seizure of power is called a 'substitution': 'crediting his own lies', he began to believe 'he was indeed the duke', and from merely playing a part he went on to become 'absolute Milan'. The figure is picked up in the comnolent dialogue of Sebastian and Antonio:

I remember
You did supplant your brother Prospero.

In the second of the scenes in which Caliban and his fellows plot to overthrow the island 'tyrant', Sebastian's 'supplant' is recalled with a difference:

Caliban. I would my valiant master would destroy thee; I do not lie.
Stephano. Trinculo, if you trouble him any more in his tale, by this hand, I will supplant some of your teeth.

The figure recurs a little later in a more serious context:

> . . . you three
> From Milan did supplant good Prospero.

In Act V after various supplantings, serious and comic, accomplished or merely projected, all true kings are restored and all false ones dethroned.

The two continuities, sovereignty-conspiracy and slavery-freedom, are also alike in the fact that their metaphorical force is expressed through scenes that are just one step removed from allegory. The more serious of the restorations and releases convey similar kinds of moral meaning. Ferdinand's release from 'wooden slavery' signifies that he is a true lover and a true prince. In being freed from madness Alonso has escaped from 'heart-sorrow' and regained his rightful rank and a 'clear life ensuing'. Both continuities convey an impression of topsyturvydom in the order of things, an unnatural interchange of status among creatures of every kind. Both express a return to stability after a disturbance of degree.

What then is the key metaphor through which the various continuities are linked, and how are they connected through it? Shakespeare's most direct expression of his key metaphor is 'sea change', the key phrase of Ariel's song. But what does Shakespeare mean by 'sea change'? Ariel sings of 'bones' being made into 'coral' and of 'eyes' becoming 'pearls'. 'A change into something rich and strange', we now understand, is a change 'out of nature'. 'Sea change' is a metaphor for 'magical transformation', for metamorphosis. The key metaphor of the play is 'change' in this special sense, and 'change' is the analogy common to all of the continuities we have been tracing. (I am not forgetting that they are also expressive of many other relationships, or that Shakespeare is often playing with two or three metaphors at once, as in the various figures of 'sea-swallowing'. But all are at least expressive of change, or changeableness.)

Through the first rather vague analogies we traced, of 'strangeness' and 'sleep-and-dream', numerous events and persons in the play are qualified as belonging to a realm where anything may happen. Expressions of 'strangeness' and 'sleep', like many of the references to sea and music, suggest 'far other Worlds and other Seas', where magical change is to be expected. A more particular metaphor of change is expressed through the stress on the 'strangeness' of 'new creations' and on the confusion between sleep and dream and waking. The island is a world of fluid, merging states of being and forms of life. This lack of dependable boundaries between states is also expressed by the many instances of confusion between natural and divine. Miranda says that she might call Ferdinand

> A thing divine; for nothing natural
> I ever saw so noble.

Ferdinand cannot be sure whether she is a goddess or a maid, and Caliban takes Trinculo for a 'brave god'. There is a further comic variation on this theme in Trinculo's difficulty in deciding whether to classify Caliban as fish or man, monster or devil.

But 'change' is most clearly and richly expressed through the sequence of tempest images (especially 'cloud' and 'sea-swallowed') and through the noise-music antithesis. All kinds of sounds, harmonious and ugly, like the manifestations of sea and storm, are expressive of magical transformation. 'The fire and cracks / Of sulfurous roaring' (imagery in which both storm and sound analogies are blended) 'infects' the courtiers' 'reason', and *solemn music* induces the 'clearing' of their understanding. The 'music' and the 'tempest' continuities, taken together as metaphors of 'sea change', are perhaps the most extensive of all the analogies in their organizing power. They recur often, they connect a wide diversity of experiences, and they express in symbolic form some of the main steps in the drama, in particular, the climactic moments of inner change: Ariel's revelation to the courtiers of their guilt, Alonso's first show of remorse, and the final purification.

The earth-air or Caliban-Ariel antithesis may seem to have very little to do with metamorphosis. But the relation of this theme to the key metaphor is clear and important. Air, Ariel, and his music are a blended symbol of change as against the unchanging Caliban, 'the thing of darkness'. He can be punished, but hardly humanized; he is, says Prospero,

> A devil, a born devil, on whose nature
> Nurture can never stick; on whom my pains,
> Humanely taken, are all lost, quite lost.

The other continuities parallel to earth-air, of slavery-freedom and conspiracy-sovereignty, are frequently expressive of major and minor changes of status among the inhabitants and temporary visitors on Prospero's island.

But the interconnection of Shakespeare's analogies through the key metaphor cannot be adequately described, since we are able to speak of only one point of relationship at a time. We can get a better sense of the felt union of various lines of analogy in *The Tempest* by looking at the two passages where Shakespeare expresses his key metaphor most completely, the 'Full fathom five' song and Prospero's 'cloud-capp'd towers' speech.

Rereading Ariel's song at this point, we can see how many of the main continuities are alluded to and related in the description of 'sea change' and how the song anticipates the metaphorical design that emerges through the dialogue of the whole play. The total metaphorical pattern is to an amazing degree an efflorescence from this single crystal:

> Full fathom five thy father lies;
> Of his bones are coral made:
> Those are pearls that were his eyes:
> Nothing of him that doth fade,
> But doth suffer a sea change
> Into something rich and strange.

> Sea nymphs hourly ring his knell:
> *Burthen:* 'Ding-dong!'
> Hark! now I hear them – Ding-dong, bell.

In addition to the more obvious references to the deep sea and its powers and to the 'strangeness' of this drowning, there are indirect anticipations of other analogies. 'Fade' prefigures the 'dissolving cloud' metaphor and the theme of tempest changes, outer and inner. 'Rich', along with 'coral' and 'pearls', anticipates the opulent imagery of the dream-world passages and scenes, the 'riches ready to drop' on Caliban and the expressions of wealth and plenty in the masque. ('Rich' and 'riches' occur no less than five times in the masque.) The song closes with the nymphs tolling the bell, the transformation and the 'sea sorrow' are expressed through sea music. Ferdinand's comment reminds us that the song has connections with two other lines of analogy:

> The ditty does remember my drown'd father.
> This is no mortal business, nor no sound
> That the earth owes: – I hear it now above me.

The song convinces Ferdinand that he is now King of Naples (the first of the interchanges of sovereignty), and it is a 'ditty' belonging not to the 'earth', but to the 'air'.

The sense of relationship between the many continuities is still more vividly felt in the lines of Prospero's most memorable speech:

> You do look, my son, in a mov'd sort,
> As if you were dismay'd: be cheerful, sir:
> Our revels now are ended. These our actors,
> As I foretold you, were all spirits and
> Are melted into air, into thin air:
> And, like the baseless fabric of this vision,
> The cloud-capp'd towers, the gorgeous palaces,
> The solemn temples, the great globe itself,
> Yea, all which it inherit, shall dissolve
> And, like this insubstantial pageant faded,
> Leave not a rack behind. We are such stuff
> As dreams are made on, and our little life
> Is rounded with a sleep.

In Prospero's words Shakespeare has gathered all the lights of analogy into a single metaphor which sums up the metaphorical design and the essential meaning of *The Tempest*. The language evokes nearly every continuity that we have traced. 'Melted into air', 'dissolve', 'cloud', and 'rack' bring us immediately to Ariel and tempest changes, while 'visions', 'dream', and 'sleep' recall other familiar continuities. 'Revels', 'gorgeous palaces', and 'pageant' (for Elizabethans closely associated with royalty) are echoes of the kingly theme; and 'solemn' is associated particularly with the soft music of change. The 'stuff' of dreams is at once cloud-stuff (air) and cloth, both images being finely compressed in 'baseless fabric'. Taken with 'faded' these images refer obliquely to the garments so miraculously 'new-dyed . . . with salt water', one of the first signs of 'sea change' noted by Gonzalo. Within the metaphor of tempest-clearing and of cloudlike transformation, Shakespeare has included allusions to every important analogy of change in the play.

But it is through the twofold progress of the whole figure that the change metaphor is experienced and its most general meaning fully understood. We read first: that like the actors and scenery of the vision, earth's glories and man shall vanish into nothingness. Through a happy mistake we also read otherwise. By the time we have passed through 'dissolve', 'insubstantial', and 'faded', and reached 'leave not a rack behind', we are reading 'cloudcapped towers' in reverse as a metaphor of tower-like clouds. 'Towers', 'palaces', 'temples', 'the great globe', 'all which it inherit' are now taken for cloud forms. Through a sort of Proustian merging of icon and subject, we experience the blending of states of being, of substantial and unsubstantial, or real and unreal, which is the essence of *The Tempest* metamorphosis.

Similar meanings are expressed through the closing dream figure, which grows equally out of the metaphorical context of the speech and the play. 'Rounded', we should take with Kittredge as 'surrounded' but without losing the force of round, as in Donne's 'surrounded with tears'. 'Our little life' is more than sentimental, it is our little life (microcosm) in contrast with 'the great globe' (macrocosm). There may also be an over-image in 'surrounded' of the world in classical myth and geography with its encircling ocean, sleep being the stream that 'rounds' the lesser world. In relation to the metaphorical design of the play, 'rounded with a sleep' and the notion of life ending in dreams express again the sense of confusion between sleep and dream and waking. This metaphor which completes the figure of cloud-change is Shakespeare's most perfect symbol for the closeness of states that to our daylight sense are easily separable. Although the vision here expressed goes far beyond the play, it is still a natural extension of the dramatic moment and a fulfillment of the metaphor that has been implicit since the noisy opening lines of *The Tempest*.

But if Shakespeare's total metaphor is in a sense present everywhere, it is also a design that develops in close relation to the main dramatic movement of the play. As we have noted more than once, a particular metaphor will be varied to fit a new dramatic situation and so serve to express the situation more fully and to anticipate the next step in the development of the drama. The best example of this adaptation of metaphor comes in a speech in which Shakespeare seems to be playing capriciously with his noise-music theme. At first sight the passage seems inconsistent with the symbolic contrast between storm noise and music:

> *Alonso.* O, it is monstrous! monstrous!
> Methought the billows spoke and told me of it;
> The winds did sing it to me; and the thunder,

That deep and dreadful organ pipe, pronounc'd
The name of Prosper: it did bass my trespass.

It is admittedly odd that the confused noise of the tempest should, in Alonso's soul, compose a harmony – however gloomy – but the paradox fits in perfectly with the developing structure of the play. Alonso has just been told by Ariel that the storm had a purpose as an instrument of Destiny. Since at this moment remorse first appears in the play and the inner clearing begins, it is exactly right that the storm should seem harmonious and so point forward to the events of the fourth and fifth acts. No use of metaphor in *The Tempest* reveals more clearly Shakespeare's exact sense of the movement of his drama, of the changing human relations and feelings he is presenting.

In building up his metaphorical design, Shakespeare prepares us for the moment in *The Tempest* when the major shift in dramatic relationships takes place. The moment comes in the speech in which Prospero describes the behavior of the King and the courtiers as they slowly return from madness to sanity. The first important step toward this climax, Alonso's acknowledgment of his guilt, was expressed through a metaphor combining both sea and musical changes. The next step, Ferdinand's release from his tempest-trials and from dreamlike enchantment, is expressed through the masque, which is an elaborate dramatization of metamorphosis, Ariel's 'meaner fellows', 'the rabble', being now transformed into majestic Olympian goddesses. Once again, familiar continuities appear, and again they are transformed to fit a new occasion. 'Earth', for example, is no longer 'barren place and fertile', but the earth enriched by human cultivation and symbolized now by Ceres – not by Caliban, who is 'nature resisting nurture'. Iris summons this new Earth in the gorgeous speech beginning 'Ceres, most bounteous lady, thy rich leas . . .', lines in which we hear a quite new majesty of tone and movement. The couplet form sets the dialogue apart from human speech, while the longer periods, the added stresses, the phrasal balancings are especially appropriate to 'that large utterance of the early gods'. (Here is one of many instances of how Shakespeare adapts his sound patterns to his metaphorical and dramatic designs.) Prospero's visionary speech that ends 'the revels' is not simply a concentration of metaphor without reference to the dramatic development. It announces the changes to come, it gives a rich expression of their meaning, and it anticipates the dreamlike flux of the psychological events of the last act.

If we now read Prospero's words in Act V, in which he describes the great changes as they take place, we see many references back to Shakespeare's metaphorical preparation for this moment. We also realize that various lines of action and various lines of analogy are converging almost simultaneously. The speech opens with Shakespeare's farewell to his art, after which he turns his thoughts to 'restoring the senses' of the courtiers, whom Ariel has just gone to release:

A solemn air and the best comforter
To an unsettled fancy, cure thy brains,
Now useless, boil'd within thy skull! There stand,

For you are spell-stopp'd.
Holy Gonzalo, honorable man,
Mine eyes, even sociable to the show of thine,
Fall fellowly drops. The charm dissolves apace;
And as the morning steals upon the night,
Melting the darkness, so their rising senses
Begin to chase the ignorant fumes that mantle
Their clearer reason. O good Gonzalo!
My true preserver, and a loyal sir
To him thou follow'st, I will pay thy graces
Home, both in word and deed. Most cruelly
Didst thou, Alonso, use me and my daughter:
Thy brother was a furtherer in the act;
Thou'rt pinch'd for 't now, Sebastian. Flesh and blood,
You, brother mine, that entertain'd ambition,
Expell'd remorse and nature; who, with Sebastian –
Whose inward pinches therefore are most strong –
Would here have kill'd your king; I do forgive thee,
Unnatural though thou art! Their understanding
Begins to swell, and the approaching tide
Will shortly fill the reasonable shores
That now lie foul and muddy. Not one of them
That yet looks on me, or would know me. Ariel,
Fetch me the hat and rapier in my cell: [*Exit* ARIEL.
I will discase me, and myself present,
As I was sometime Milan. Quickly, spirit;
Thou shalt ere long be free.

If this is a climactic moment, what changes in dramatic relationships are
taking place, what is happening dramatically? The 'men of sin', like Ferdinand, have come to the end of the trials which began with the storm and
continued through various 'distractions'. Now, as Prospero explains, they are
undergoing a moral as well as a mental regeneration, they are 'pinch'd' with
remorse and are being forgiven. The twofold regeneration is further
dramatized in the speeches that follow: 'th' affliction of Alonso's mind
amends', he resigns Prospero's dukedom and 'entreats' him to pardon his
'wrongs'.

But these are the prose facts, the bare bones of the changes in dramatic
relationships. We cannot feel the peculiar quality of what is taking place or
grasp its meaning apart from the metaphorical language through which it is
being expressed. And the expressions acquire their force and precision from
the whole metaphorical preparation we have been tracing. The courtiers'
senses are restored by 'an airy charm', by magic similar to that which was
worked by Ariel and his spirits. The allusions to 'heavenly music' and 'a
solemn air', in contrast to the 'rough magic' that Prospero has abjured, remind
us that these changes will be musically harmonious, like the songs of Ariel,

and not noisy and confused like the storm sent to punish these men and reveal their 'monstrous' guilt. Towards the end of the speech, the imagery recalls the tempest metaphor, but it is altered so as to express the mental and moral change that is taking place. The return of understanding is like an approaching tide that covers the evidence of a storm (both 'foul' and 'muddy' have storm associations from earlier occurrences).

But the metaphor that best expresses this clearing is the one for which the preparation has been most complete:

> The charm dissolves apace;
> And as the morning steals upon the night,
> Melting the darkness, so their rising senses
> Begin to chase the ignorant fumes that mantle
> Their clearer reason.

'Dissolving' and 'melting' and 'fumes' take us back at once to the grand transformations of the masque speech, to the earlier cloud transformations both serious and comic; and they take us back further to the association of clouds with magical tempests, inner storms, and clearing weather. We read of the moral and psychological transformations with a present sense of these analogies. They are qualified for us as a dreamlike dissolution of tempest clouds, as events in the 'insubstantial' region where reality and unreality merge.

It is through such links that Shakespeare concentrates at this climactic moment the fullest meaning of his key metaphor. There is, of course, no separation in the reader's experience between the dramatic fact and the metaphorical qualification. The images that recur in Prospero's speech take us back to felt qualities, but to felt qualities embedded in particular dramatic contexts. 'Melting', for example, carries us to the spiritlike dissolution of 'spirits . . . melted into air, into thin air'; but it also reminds us of the masque pageantry and of Prospero's calming of Ferdinand's fears. We hear Prospero's soothing and mysterious tone in both the earlier and later uses of the word. The dramatic links and the analogical links are experienced at once, which is to say that metaphorical design and dramatic design are perfectly integrated.

We can now realize that metamorphosis is truly the key metaphor to the *drama,* and not the key metaphor to a detachable design of decorative analogies. Through the echoes in Prospero's speech of various lines of analogy, Prospero makes us feel each shift in dramatic relationships as a magical transformation, whether it is the courtiers' return to sanity, or Prospero's restoration to his dukedom, or Ariel's flight into perpetual summer. While all of the 'slaves' and 'prisoners' are being freed, and while all of the 'sovereigns' are being restored, the sense of magical change is never wholly lost. The union of drama and metaphor in *The Tempest* is nowhere more complete than in the last act of the play.

The larger meaning of Shakespeare's total design, which was anticipated in the cloud and dream metaphor of Prospero's visionary speech, is most clearly and fully expressed in these final transformations. In a world where everywhere may become something else, doubts naturally arise, and in the swift flow of change the confusion about what is and what is not becomes fairly acute. When Prospero 'discases' himself and appears as Duke of Milan, Gonzalo says with understandable caution:

> Whether this be,
> Or be not, I'll not swear

And Prospero answers:

> You do yet taste
> Some subtilties o' the isle, that will not let you
> Believe things certain.

Whereas in the earlier acts the characters had often accepted the unreal as real (spirits, shipwrecks, drownings, visions), they now find it difficult to accept the real as truly real. The play concludes with their acceptance of the unexpected change to reality. But for the spectator there remains the heightened sense of the 'thin partitions' that 'do divide' these states. The world that common sense regards as real, of order in nature and society and of sanity in the individual, is a shimmering transformation of disorder. 'We shall all be changed, in a moment, in the twinkling of an eye.' (This or something like it is as near as we can come to describing the total attitude conveyed by *The Tempest.)*

Thus *The Tempest* is, like Marvell's 'Garden', a Metaphysical poem of metamorphosis, though the meaning of change is quite different for the two writers. It is worth noting too that Shakespeare 'had Ovid in his eye', a fact that is obvious from the echoes of Golding's famous translation. There could be no better proof of Shakespeare's maturity than the contrast between the 'sweet witty' Ovidianism of 'Venus and Adonis' and the metaphorical design of *The Tempest*, which gives philosophic meaning to a drama of Ovidian metamorphosis. We remember 'a lily prison'd in a jail of snow' as an isolated 'beauty', but hardly as an apt symbol of the amorous relations of Venus and Adonis, or as symbolic of some larger meaning in their story. (Indeed a 'jail of snow' is rather inept for the fervid goddess of the poem.) 'Those were pearls that were his eyes' revives Ariel's sea music, Ferdinand's melancholy, and a world of fantasy and transshifting states of being. The increased concentration in meaning of the image from *The Tempest* is a sign of a growth in the command of language which is command of life for a poet. As Arnold said of Wordsworth, Shakespeare now 'deals with more of *life*' and 'he deals with *life*, as a whole, more powerfully'. His maturity and power appear in the variety of experience so perfectly harmonized through the imaginative design of *The Tempest*.

By Reuben A. Brower

Notes

[1]The music and tempest metaphors have been traced in a very different fashion and with quite different aims by G. Wilson Knight in *The Shakespearian Tempest* (1932). My analysis (which I

had worked out before reading Professor Knight's essay) has a more limited purpose: to show a continuity of analogy and a development of metaphor parallel to that of the other continuities I have traced.

[2]The scene is full of expressions such as: *A tempestuous noise of thunder and lightning heard*, 'roarers', 'command these elements of silence', *A cry within*, 'A plague upon this howling! they are louder than the weather, or our office', 'insolent noisemaker', *A confused noise within*, etc.

Selected Criticisms

There is in *The Tempest* the solemn tone of a testament. It might be said that, before his death, the poet, in this epopee of the ideal, had designed a codicil for the Future. In this enchanted isle, full of 'sounds and sweet airs that give delight,' we may expect to behold Utopia, the promised land of future generations, Paradise regained. Who in reality is Prospero, the king of this isle? Prospero is the shipwrecked sailor who reaches port, the exile who regains his native land, he who from the depths of despair becomes all-powerful, the worker who by his science has tamed matter, Caliban, and by his genius spirit, Ariel. Prospero is man, the master of Nature and the despot of destiny; he is the man-Providence!

The Tempest is the supreme denouement, dreamed by Shakespeare, for the bloody drama of Genesis. It is the expiation of the primordial crime. The region whither it transports us is the enchanted land where the sentence of damnation is absolved by clemency, and where reconciliation is ensured by amnesty to the fratricide. And, at the close of the piece, when the poet, touched by emotion, throws Antonio into the arms of Prospero, he has made Cain pardoned by Abel.

Francois-Victor Hugo

If I read *The Tempest* rightly, it is an example of how a great poet should write allegory, not embodying meta-physical abstractions, but giving us ideals abstracted from life itself, suggesting an under-meaning everywhere, forcing it upon us nowhere, tantalizing the mind with hints that imply so much and tell so little, and yet keep the attention all eye and ear with eager, if fruitless, expectation. Here the leading characters are not merely typical, but symbolical, that is, they do not illustrate a class of persons, they belong to universal Nature. . . . There is scarce a play of Shakespeare's in which there is such variety of character, none in which character has so little to do in the carrying on and development of the story. But consider for a moment if ever the Imagination has been so embodied as in Prospero, the Fancy as in Ariel, the brute Understanding as in Caliban, who, the moment his poor wits are warmed with the glorious liquor of Stephano, plots rebellion against his natural lord, the higher Reason. Miranda is mere abstract Womanhood, as truly so before she sees Ferdinand as Eve before she was wakened to consciousness by the echo of her own nature coming back to her, the same, and yet not the same, from that of Adam. Ferdinand, again, is nothing more than Youth, compelled to drudge at something he despises, till the sacrifice of will

and abnegation of self win him his ideal in Miranda. The subordinate personages are simply types; Sebastian and Antonio, of weak character and evil
ambition; Gonzalo, of average sense and honesty; Adrian and Francisco, of
the walking gentlemen who fill up a world. They are not characters in the same
sense with Iago, Falstaff, Shallow, or Leontes; and it is curious how every one
of them loses his way in this enchanted island of life, all the victims of one
illusion after another, except Prospero, whose ministers are purely ideal. The
whole play indeed is a succession of illusions, winding up with those solemn
words of the great enchanter who had summoned to his service every shape of
merriment or passion, every figure in the great tragi-comedy of life, and who
was now bidding farewell to the scene of his triumphs. For in Prospero shall
we not recognize the Artist himself,

> 'That did not better for his life provide
> Than public means which public manners breeds,
> Whence comes it that his name receives a brand,'

who has forfeited a shining place in the world's eye by devotion to his art, and
who turned adrift on the ocean of life on the leaky carcass of a boat, has
shipwrecked on that Fortunate Island (as men always do who find their true
vocation), where he is absolute lord, making all the powers of Nature serve
him, but with Ariel and Caliban as special ministers?

James Russell Lowell

The music of the spheres is not referred to specifically as such in 'The
Tempest,' but the whole play is concerned as taking part on an island that
resounds continually to music in the air, which is, I believe, equivalent to
music of the spheres. The island governed by the benevolent power of
Prospero is in itself a type of the golden-age island, where no ill is ultimately
allowed, where strife and friction are allayed and everything is to be wrapped
in a serene air of celestial harmony. The terrible discord of the storm with its
tempestuous noise of thunder and its fearful flash of lightning at the very
beginning of the play is indicative of the discord that has been perpetrated in
the microcosmos. Prospero and Miranda have been deposed from their lawful
state and the deposers are now brought to Prospero's island. By music's power
he is able to resolve his problems one by one and harmony is restored.

John P. Cutts

When one is travelling through that wild terrain of criticism relating to
Shakespeare's last plays, there is very little upon which to rely. One is faced
with a thousand questions – Are the plays myth, romance, or an elaborate
working out of the tragic pattern? Were they written because the poet wished
to return to the forms he had used in youth, because he was bored, or because
he was pandering to the tastes of a new audience? Is *The Tempest* a pastoral
drama, a dramatic rendition of masque and anti-masque, or a religious
parable? To each question there is a most ingeniously contrived reply. But,
however sharply the critics disagree in their interpretations of *The Tempest*,

there are two points upon which they stand together almost to a man. The first is that the last plays must be considered together; as Tillyard puts it, *The Tempest* 'gains much in lucidity when supported by the others'.[1] The second point of agreement is that all of the last plays are concerned with the theme of regeneration, and that *The Tempest* realizes this theme most perfectly. It is upon these two points, I think, that the critics are most completely in error. *The Tempest* does not gain in being considered as part of a thematic whole that includes the others, rather its meaning becomes obscured in such a context. And the first error of tying the plays together leads inevitably to the second; it is always after a recapitulation of Thaisa's resurrection from the sea and Hermione's revival from the dead that the critics make an unjustifiable extension of the regeneration theory to include *The Tempest*. It is their unshaken belief that regeneration is the theme of the play that makes them slide over the key speech,

> Our revels now are ended: these our actors –
> As I foretold you – were all spirits and
> Are melted into air, into thin air;
> And like the baseless fabric of this vision
> The cloud-capped towers, the gorgeous palaces,
> The solemn temples, the great globe itself
> Yea, all which it inherit, shall dissolve
> And like this insubstantial pageant faded
> Leave not a rack behind; we are such stuff
> As dreams are made on, and our little life
> Is rounded with a sleep.

This speech and the epilogue sound the keynote, but it is a note that jars with the triumphant harmony that the last plays are thought to express.

The meaning of *The Tempest* can best be approached if we contrast it with the other late plays. The most immediately perceptible difference between *The Tempest* and the romances is structural. Almost all critics of the play remark upon the closeness with which Shakespeare adheres to classical formulae in this work, a method both contrary to the poet's usual practice and almost inimical to the traditional structure of romance. For example, the unities of time, place, and action are preserved. Exposition of past action and the presentation of all the characters (except Stephano and Trinculo) occur before the end of the first act. The second act introduces the disturbance that must be resolved by the end of the play. In the third act the turbulence is intensified according to the formula for epitasis. The fourth act continues the epitasis with the threatened revolt of Caliban, but it also prepares for the comic ending with the union of the lovers. The peculiar insistence of the poet upon the classical structure becomes obvious at this point. As Kermode notes, 'The apparently unnecessary perturbation at the thought of Caliban may be a point at which an oddly pedantic concern for classical structure causes it to force its way through the surface of the play'.[2] . . . . one must agree with Kermode that here as well as elsewhere in the play, the rigorous formality of the structure forces itself upon the reader's attention. It is a fact impossible to ignore that Shakespeare deliberately constructed the play in accordance with neo-Terentian rules. But why, one is led to ask, did he choose so formal a structure in dealing with the extravagant materials of romance? Clifford Leech, in his article on the structure of the last plays has an interesting idea that may shed light on this strange paradox. The last plays, he says, deal not with single, limited incidents, as the comedies and tragedies, for example, do. Rather, they deal with situations that follow upon one another in haphazard concurrence with the flux that is the governing pattern in actual life. That is, in the last plays the beginnings and endings of the plays are not inevitable, but are arbitrarily set, so that we could imagine the characters having more adventures after the ending of the play. In *The Tempest,* because of the controlling magic of Prospero, the flux is arrested, but it remains as part of the undercurrent of the play, 'in contrapuntal relationship to the act-structure'.[3] This idea, when it is pursued, can lead us to the heart of the play, for the theme of *The Tempest* is not regeneration through suffering, but the eternal conflict between order and chaos, the attempt of art to impose form upon the formless and chaotic, and the limitations of art in this endeavor.

In proving this hypothesis, it might be well to begin with an examination of the character of Prospero and the relation of the other characters to him. Prospero is not, as Tillyard would have him, a king who has made a tragic mistake and then repented it, nor is he Wilson Knight's superman, nor Churton Collins' idea of God. It would be going too far to say, with D. G. James, that Prospero is a poet and Ariel his imagination; but without falling into an allegorical interpretation we can safely say that Prospero is an artist of a kind. He uses music, the very symbol of order, in creating his effects, he attempts to manipulate the other characters to the end of creating or preserving order and form. We can say that for Prospero, as for the poet who is creating the play, all time is present and all the action fore-known to and controlled by him. However, to counterbalance this image, which by itself might well cause a critic to mistake him for God, Prospero is also at times irascible, at times a bit ridiculous, and always under necessity to combat those forces of disorder which he cannot control. We might outline his role in this way: Prospero at the beginning of the play is in a position in which he can take his enemies (who represent disordered mankind, since they are usurpers) out of the flux of life – which is emphasized by their voyage from a marriage feast back to the affairs of state. His enemies are Antonio and Sebastian, the center of the forces of disorder, and Alonso and Ferdinand, who will be permanently influenced by their experience; with them is Gonzalo, who already stands on the side of the forces of order. Prospero will place the travellers on an enchanted island which he controls almost completely through order and harmony – I say almost because he cannot wholly bring Caliban, the incarnation of chaos, into his system of order. He takes Alonso, Antonio, and Co. out of the flux of life and into a kind of permanence, a change which Ariel describes:

Full fadom five thy father lies

Of his bones are coral made
Those are pearls that were his eyes
Nothing of him that doth fade
But doth suffer a sea-change
Into something rich and strange.

The process is not one of regeneration into something more nobly human, and despite the interest of the Twentieth Century in Frazer's *Golden Bough*, there is nothing here that suggests fertility, rather the human and impermanent is transfixed into a rich permanence, but a lifeless one. Potentially corruptible bones and eyes become incorruptible coral and pearls; form and richness are fixed upon what was changing and subject to decay. Prospero takes the travellers out of the world of change and places them on his enchanted island, which is permeated with an ordering harmony. Caliban describes the effect of the harmony upon him,

Sometimes a thousand twangling instruments
Will hum about mine ears, and sometimes voices
That if I waked after long sleep
Will make me sleep again, and then in dreaming
The clouds methought would open and show riches
Ready to drop upon me, that when I wak'd
I cried to dream again.

This harmony first renders the animate inanimate and then reveals riches. Prospero will subject the travellers to the ordering influence of his art. Upon some of them he will impose an order that (we suppose) will stay with them even after they have returned to the world of change, some of them will be influenced only for the moment, as Caliban in the passage quoted, because they are agents of disorder. But in the end, all of them, even Prospero once he has abandoned his art, will have to return to the world of mutability.

I have said that Prospero is an artist who controls through his art. There is no suspense in the play because Prospero can control future as well as present action. His foreknowledge enables him to control all that occurs within the confines of the play. Kermode says that ' . . . the qualities of the poor isle which gave [the characters] new birth, which purged Alonso's guilt and taught the princely skill to submit his fury to his reason, are the main theme of the play' (p. xxx). But the qualities of the isle have nothing to do with Prospero's art. In the exposition he tells us that he brought his art with him to the island, that Sycorax, the very mother of chaos, had employed the qualities of the island before Prospero's art brought them under the control of form and order. Nor can we believe that Prospero has yet to bring his fury under the control of reason. If he really had to wait for Ariel to persuade him to mercy, would he have arranged the union of his daughter with Ferdinand? Prospero has already brought order to himself and his island before the play opens. In the play he will take disordered men out of the world and place them under a control that has already been established. There is no real conflict in Prospero's world and therefore no suspense. The play is not one in which the theme evolves, it is rather displayed. The characters who are, as Pettet suggests,[4] more than half pasteboard, are lined up as representatives of order or disorder. Open conflict between the two forces never really occurs, but we are shown the ways in which chaos is always threatening to overflow the boundaries which form has set upon it. And finally we are shown by Prospero the nature and limitations of his art.

We must first discuss the forces of order and the forces of chaos as they are lined up in the scheme of the play. Prospero, of course, is the center of order, but Ferdinand and Miranda, under his tutelage, become agents of order, and Gonzalo represents an order of his own which exists even before he is manipulated by Prospero. It is significant that the images of an orderer and creator are applied to Gonzalo as well as to Prospero. For instance, in the scene where we first encounter Gonzalo, Antonio and Sebastian are mocking him thus,

> *Ant.* His words are more than the miraculous harp
> *Seb.* He hath raised the wall and houses too.
> *Ant.* What impossible matter will he make easy next?
> *Seb.* I think he will carry this island home in his pocket and give it to his son for an apple.
> *Ant.* And sowing kernels of it in the sea, will bring forth more apples.
> *Gon.* [having pondered] Aye.

Gonzalo, who we are told in the exposition was the one man who aided the exiled Prospero, is described by the men who mock him as a builder, a planter of seeds. It is true that he is a comic character; much of what he says is ridiculous. But the desire for order in a world governed by change is, to an extent, ridiculous. Prospero lives on an enchanted island where his word is law. Gonzalo lives in a world of mutability, governed by agents of disorder, like Antonio. His dream of order in such a world is bound to seem ridiculous. It is significant, however, that Gonzalo is made to long for the return of a golden age.

> . . . treason, felony,
> Sword, pike, knife, gun or need of any engine
> Would I not have; but Nature should bring forth
> Of its own kind all foison, all abundance
> To feed my innocent people.

Preposterous as it is, his account of an ideal kingdom makes its point. His fantasy is, at least, constructive; the chaffing of Antonio and Sebastian, destructive. There are two tests provided in the play that distinguish the advocates of order from the agents of disorder: obedience to laws governing political order, and obedience to laws governing personal, emotional order.

The emphasis that Prospero puts upon chastity and the santity of marriage has been interpreted as an indication that this play is a kind of elaborate fertility rite, or that a new, more mature love relationship is being considered here. But the love of Ferdinand and Miranda, as love, is unimportant. The lovers hardly come alive as characters, there is little actual wooing involved, and since we know from the beginning that Prospero approves of the match, suspense plays no part in our reaction to the love affair. But why should Prospero impose the rather meaningless task of log-carrying upon Ferdinand, and why should he be so insistent in urging the lovers to be chaste until the marriage ceremony is performed? Surely in comedy or romance the audience takes for granted that the lovers will be chaste until the wedding day. If there were to be some conflict involved, some reason to suspect that they would break, or at least be tempted to break, their promise to Prospero, this would be sufficient reason for the emphasis that he puts upon their vow of chastity. But Ferdinand and Miranda are so obviously chaste, so obviously obedient, that one questions why the issue should be raised at all. The answer is that ceremony, vows, all attempts to train human behavior to order are important. Ferdinand is made to carry logs, not because log-carrying is necessary, but because he must submit himself to the discipline of a test to win Miranda. He must submit will and pride to order, and when he does, Prospero gives him Miranda as 'thine own acquisition / Worthily purchased'. Chastity before marriage is necessary because it is part of the formal code to which human beings must submit that life may be meaningfully ordered. Ferdinand vows chastity in the hope of gaining 'quiet days, fair issue and long life', a good and orderly existence, not wildly romantic love. He promises not 'to take the edge off the [wedding] day's celebration'. The emphasis is not upon love, nor upon fertility, but upon order, ritual, ceremony.

However, the emphasis is not achieved through action (Ferdinand's trial is purposely made the dull chore of carrying logs) but through contrast. If Gonzalo, Ferdinand and Miranda, with Prospero in the fore, are the creators of and submitters to a system of order, Antonio and Sebastian, Stephano and Trinculo, with Caliban in the center, are creators of disorder. Again the two qualities that distinguish them as agents of chaos are sexual intemperance and the refusal to submit to political authority. Since Caliban is the very incarnation of chaos and an active creator of disorder (as Prospero is of order) it may be well to consider him first. Kermode has said that Caliban is the natural man, unqualified for nurture and existing on the simplest level of sensual pain and pleasure. But Caliban is not just nature stripped of grace and civility, he is unnatural; he is not simply unformed nature, he is deformed. He is not only incapable of receiving form, but he is also potentially able and eager to extend his own disordered nature. To begin with, Caliban is not a pastoral figure, a natural inhabitant of the island. He is not a man at all, but is 'legged like a man and his fins like arms', He is an unnatural half-man, half-fish. His very birth was inhuman, for his mother was Sycorax, a witch, and his father was the devil; he is, therefore, the offspring of active malignancy. G. Wilson Knight has said that Caliban is part of Prospero's nature, basing his arguments upon the speech at the end of the play wherein Prospero "owns" Caliban. But Caliban is not part of Prospero, he comprises that element of the disordered that Prospero's art cannot reach, and Prospero claims him as a deficiency or limitation of his art. Caliban is actively opposed to Prospero's order. Prospero cannot enchant him into goodness, he controls him with agues and pinches. Caliban is a 'lying slave / Whom stripes may move not kindness'. At times he can be enchanted by the harmony of the island, but only for brief moments. Prospero's order must be constantly enforced and preserved against the ever-threatening encroachment of Caliban's disorder. It is significant that it is those very bulwarks of order, temperance and obedience, those qualities which Prospero so insistently exacts from Miranda and Ferdinand, which Caliban's disordered nature resists. In the first scene in which the monster appears we learn that his past response to the ordering influence of Prospero has been an attempt to ravish Miranda. His thwarted design is the desire to 'people . . . this isle with Calibans', almost a symbol of chaos threatening to overwhelm order. The idea recurs when Caliban promises Stephano that Miranda 'will bring thee forth brave brood'. Just as Ferdinand's obedience to order promises to reward him, after due ceremony and in proper time, with 'fair issue', so Caliban's rebellion against order threatens to people the isle with monsters or drunken usurpers. This brings us to the second manifestation of Caliban's disordered nature, rebellion. G. Wilson Knight's description is apt. Caliban, he says, 'symbolizes all brainless revolution such as Jack Cade's in *Henry VI* Part II, and the absurdity of the mob mentality in *Julius Caesar* and *Coriolanus*'.[5] The whole scene with Stephano and Trinculo is an exquisite parody of the power-quest theme. Stephano's attempts at high diction, 'by this hand I will supplant some of thy teeth', and 'the poor monster's my subject and he shall not suffer indignity', are delightfully comic. But there is a serious undertone throughout. Caliban's mistaking a drunken churl for a god, the alacrity with which he would exchange worth for worthlessness,

> A plague upon the tyrant that I serve!
> I'll bear him no more sticks, but follow thee
> Thou wondrous man.

But more important is the unrelenting malignancy of Caliban. Stephano and Trinculo are clowns who are drunken and silly; they can be diverted from their usurpation by the sight of a few glittering garments, but Caliban's is an active evil. He prods them to their task constantly with, 'When Prospero's destroyed', and 'Let's alone and do the murther first'. His will is set upon the destruction of order and goodness even when he has almost nothing to gain from his revolt, for he is, after all, merely exchanging one master for another. He has promised the same service to Stephano that he had begrudged Prospero, 'I'll pluck thee berries / I'll fish for thee, and get thee wood enough'. His expected freedom is illusory for he has already pledged himself to slavery. His desire then is for the destruction of order and the creation of chaos.

Just as Gonzalo represents Prospero's kind of order as it appears in the world outside of the enchanted island, so Antonio represents Caliban's kind of disorder as it appears in life. Antonio, like Caliban, promotes evil for its own sake. He has nothing to gain from the usurpation by Sebastian of Alonso's throne, yet he prods Sebastian into rebellion and attempted murder for the sake of disrupting order. G. Wilson Knight finds countless verbal and imagistic echoes of *Macbeth* in the scheming of Antonio with Sebastian. This scene, by recalling the tragedies and histories, achieves a seriousness of tone that is rather startling in the atmosphere of the enchanted island. The serious undercurrent that runs through the Caliban-Stephano-Trinculo scenes here breaks the comic surface, and evil for its own sake, the urge of disorder to extend itself, stands fully revealed. Of course, Prospero's magic can control this manifestation of disorder; Ariel wakes Alonso, and all the travellers are put under a spell; but this control is only temporary. As Wilson Knight says, '. . . poetic honesty leaves Antonio's final reformation doubtful' (p. 213).

This brings us to the final question considered by the theme, the limitations of art in imposing order upon chaos. Prospero is a great artist, as we have said, but he is not to be confused with God. He has limitations. In the first place, he is mortal. His great art is a power which is not constant but which is assumed and which must finally be abandoned. Prospero's humanness is revealed to us at the very beginning of the play in two different scenes. The first is that in which he is revealing his past history to an almost completely inattentive Miranda. 'Dost thou attend me?' he asks. 'Thou attend'st not', he gently chides. 'I pray thee, mark me', he insists. A slight diminution from the great magician to dear old Daddy occurs here. But in the scene with Ariel where the mighty magician threatens the wisp of a spirit, 'If thou murmur'st, I will rend an oak / And peg thee in his knotty entrails till / Thou hast howl'd away twelve winters', Prospero earns the name that many critics have bestowed upon him of a crusty and irascible old pedant.

But though the artist is proved a man, that does not answer the question of the limitations of his art. What, we must ask ourselves, does Prospero's art finally accomplish? It has established an ordered future for Ferdinand and Miranda; it has wrought a permanent change upon Alonso; but it has not been able to touch the deeply disordered natures of Antonio and Sebastian and it had never been able to fix form upon Caliban. Prospero's art then can order what is amenable to order, but it can only affect temporarily that which is fundamentally chaotic. . . . The will, the refusal to submit to order, is at the center of the evil that cannot be reached by Prospero's art.

Prospero is himself aware of the limitations of his art. The masque which has been the jumping-off place for so many of the theories that would describe the play as a fertility celebration, is, we are told by Prospero, only the enactment of his wishes for the blessing of an ordered life upon Ferdinand and Miranda. He describes the figures in the masque as,

> Spirits which by mine art
> I have from their confines called to enact
> My present fancies.

The masque reveals Prospero's desire for order and goodness, but his wish cannot be realized unless those upon whom he wishes this blessing themselves desire it. The masque is simply the projection of Prospero's imagination; it shows its frailty by dissolving when the great artist thinks of something else.

The stage directions are quite explicit at this point. 'They join with the nymphs in a graceful dance, toward the end whereof Prospero starts suddenly and speaks, after which to a strange hollow and confused noise, they heavily vanish'. Prospero tells us that they are airy nothing, and as they vanish, he warns, all the endeavors of men at creation, palaces, cloud-capped towers, solemn temples are doomed to fade away. It is significant too that it is the recollection of Caliban, the threat of disorder and the coming of chaos, that drives the masque into thin air. The order influence of art can throw up only temporary bulwarks against change, disorder and decay. Prospero is fated, at last, to abandon his art and his enchanted island and to return to being a mere man in a world of change, facing final decay:

> Now my charms are all o'erthrown
> And what strength I have's my own
> Which is most faint . . .
>
> . . . Now I want
> Spirits to enforce, art to enchant
> And my ending is despair
> Unless I be reliev'd by prayer . . .

Only in a world of art, an enchanted island, or the play itself, does order arrest mutability and control disorder; but art must at last be abandoned, and then nothing is left mankind but to sue for grace.

Rose Abdelnour Zimbardo

Notes

1. E. M. W. Tillyard, *Shakespeare's Last Plays* (1954) p. 49.
2. Frank Kermode, Introduction to *The Tempest* (New Arden ed.: 1954) p. lxxv.
3. Clifford Leech, 'The Structure of the Last Plays', in *Shakespeare Survey*, II (1958), p. 27.
4. E. C. Pettet, *Shakespeare and the Romance Tradition* (New York, 1949).
5. G. Wilson Knight, *The Crown of Life* (1947) p. 211.

The Tempest has two endings: a quiet evening on the island, when Prospero forgives his enemies and the story returns to the point of departure; and Prospero's tragic monologue, spoken directly to the audience, a monologue out of time. But *The Tempest* also possesses two prologues. The first of these is the dramatic one; it takes place on the ship, which is set on fire by lightning and tossed on the rocks by the wind. The other prologue consists of Prospero's account of how he had lost his dukedom and came to live on the uninhabited island; it narrates the previous history of the *dramatis personae*.

On the surface, the first prologue – like Prospero's closing monologue – seems unnecessary. It takes place out of the island and only provides, as it were, a frame. But it serves a double dramatic purpose. It shows a real tempest, as distinguished from the inner storm, from the madness which will overcome the characters in view of the audience. It is only after the physical and material tempest has been depicted that the morality will be performed.

All that happens on the island will be a play within a play, a performance produced by Prospero.

But this dramatic prologue has one other purpose. It is a direct exposition of one of the great Shakespearian theses, a violent confrontation of nature with the social order. The ship carries a king. What is royal might and majesty when confronted with raging elements? Nothing. Shakespeare repeats Panurge's famous invocation from the fourth book of *Gargantua and Pantagruel,* but how much more sharply and strongly he does it.

Gonzalo. Nay, good, be patient.
Boatswain. When the sea is. Hence! What cares these roarers for the
name of king? To cabin: silence! Trouble us not.
Gonzalo. Good, yet remember whom thou hast aboard.
Boatswain. None that I more love than myself. You are a counsellor; if you can command these elements to silence, and work
the peace of the present, we will not hand a rope more; use your
authority: if you cannot, give thanks you have lived so
long . . .

(Act I, Sc. 1)

This in a nutshell, and in a condensed form, is the theme of *King Lear*.

In the prologue to *The Tempest,* the deprivation of majesty's sacred character – so characteristic of the Renaissance – is realized once more. Faced with the roaring sea, a boatswain means more than a king.

Now for Prospero's account, which is the other prologue to *The Tempest*. It is a long account and seems to include some undigested elements of an old play from which Shakespeare has probably taken the plot. It is of no importance. Prospero's story takes up one of the main, basic – almost obsessional – Shakespearian themes: that of a good and a bad ruler, of the usurper who deprives the legal prince of his throne. This is Shakespeare's view of history, eternal history, its perpetual, unchanging mechanism. It is repeated in the Histories and in the Tragedies – in *Hamlet* and *Macbeth* – even in the comedies, for this theme is present in *Measure for Measure* and in *As You Like It*. Only in the Roman tragedies, although the mechanism of history and of the struggle for power remains the same, are the *dramatis personae* different; they include the senate and the people, the patricians, tribunes and army generals.

In Prospero's narrative the framework of feudal history is bare, purged of all allegory and chance, almost deprived of names and character; it is abstract like a formula. Prospero's account is a summary of Machiavelli's treatise, *The Prince*.

. . . the liberal arts,
. . . being all my study,
The government I cast upon my brother,
And to my state grew stranger . . .
. . . They false uncle –
Being once perfected how to grant suits,

How to deny them, who t'advance, and who
To trash for over-topping, new created
The creatures that were mine . . .
     . . . set all hearts i'the state
To what tune pleas'd his ear; that now he was
The ivy which had hid my princely trunk,
And suck'd my verdure out on't.

To have no screen between this part he play'd
And him he play'd it for, he needs will be
Absolute Milan.

       . . . confederates –
      . . . . with the King of Naples
To give him annual tribute, do him homage.

       . . . one midnight
    . . . did . . . open
The gates of Milan . . .

(Act I, Sc. 2)

Prospero's narrative is a description of a struggle for power, of violence and conspiracy. But it applies not only to the dukedom of Milan. The same theme will be repeated in the story of Ariel and Caliban. Shakespeare's theatre is the *Theatrum Mundi*. Violence, as the principle on which the world is based, will be shown in cosmic terms. The previous history of Ariel and Caliban is a repetition of Prospero's history, another illustration of the same theme. Shakespearian dramas are constructed not on the principle of unity of action, but on the principle of analogy, comprising a double, treble, or quadruple plot, which repeats the same basic theme; they are a system of mirrors, as it were, both concave and convex, which reflect, magnify and parody the same situation.[1] The same theme returns in various keys, in all the registers of Shakespeare's music; it is repeated lyrically and grotesquely, then pathetically and ironically. The same situation will be performed on the Shakespearian stage by kings, then repeated by lovers and aped by clowns. Or is it the kings who ape the clowns? Kings, lovers, clowns are all actors. Parts are written and situations given. So much the worse, if the actors are not suited for their parts and cannot play them properly. For they perform on a stage which depicts the real world, where no-one chooses his or her part, or situation. Situations in Shakespearian theatre are always real, even when interpreted by ghosts and monsters.

    Even before the sea-currents took the raft, carrying Miranda and Prospero, to the island, the first act of violence and terror had already taken place. Ariel had been captured by the witch Sycorax and – for refusing to obey her abominable orders – imprisoned in a cloven pine-tree. He suffered, for until then he had been free as air. 'Thou wast a spirit too delicate to act her earthy and abhorr'd commands' – as Prospero will tell him. Prospero liberates Ariel, but only to make him serve, to make him obey his own power. Shakespeare is always in a hurry to state the conflict and situations, abruptly and at once. No sooner has Prospero ended his narrative, and Ariel given his account of the shipwreck, than the conflict breaks out with full force. The prologue is over; action has begun. . . .

The theme of force has already been introduced twice. But on the island there is another character of the drama: Caliban. The same theme, the same situation will be repeated for the third time. Only the parts will be reversed and Shakespeare will introduce a new mirror. This time it will be a crooked mirror. Caliban is the offspring of Sycorax's union with the devil. On her death he assumed rule of the island. He was its rightful lord, at least in the feudal sense. Caliban lost his realm, just as Prospero had lost his dukedom. Caliban was overthrown by Prospero, just as Prospero had been overthrown by Antonio. Even before the morality proper is performed, and Prospero's enemies undergo the trial of madness, two acts of feudal history have already been played out on the desert island.

> *Caliban.* This island's mine, by Sycorax my mother,
> Which thou tak'st from me. When thou camest first,
> Thou strok'dst me, and made much of me; wouldst give me
> Water with berries in't . . .
> . . . I. . .
>
> . . . first was mine own king. . . .
>
> (Act I, Sc. 2)

Caliban's first revolt still belongs to the antecedents of the drama. Caliban assaulted Miranda and tried to rape her. His attempt failed. Caliban was confined to a cave, forced to carry wood and water, and suffer torture consisting of cramps, aches, pricks. Shakespeare is a master of literality. Ariel's sufferings are abstract, and the liberty he seeks is abstract too. It is a rejection of all forms of dependence. Caliban's sufferings are concrete, physical, animal. Characters in Shakespearian dramas are never introduced by chance. The first scene in which Ariel appears brings a demand for liberty. The first appearance of Caliban marks a recollection of revolt. It is the entry of a slave. The cruelty of this scene is wholly deliberate; so is its brutal materialistic quality.

> *Prospero.* Thou poisonous slave, got by the devil himself
> Upon thy wicked dam, come forth!
> *Caliban.* As wicked dew – as e'er my mother brush'd
> With raven's feather from unwholesome fen,
> Drop on you both! a south-west blow on ye,
> And blister you all o'er!
>
> (Act I, Sc. 2)

The exposition is over. Such are the life-stories of the inhabitants of a desert island, on the rocky shores of which the ship carrying Prospero's old enemies has been wrecked.

For most commentators the island in *The Tempest* is a utopia, or a fairy isle. Let us look at it more closely, as it is going to be the scene of the drama proper. Where does this island lie, what does it signify, and how has Shakespeare described it?

From the itinerary of the sea-voyage undertaken by Alonso, King of Naples, who is returning from Tunis, and from the story of the witch Sycorax, who had come to the island from Algiers, it follows that Prospero's island should be situated in the Mediterranean. At the cross-roads of both routes lies Malta. Other commentators place the island nearer to Sicily and think it is the rocky Pantelleria. Still others are of the opinion that the island lies near the shore of North Africa and take it to be Lampedusa. But Setebos, whom the witch Sycorax worshipped, was a god of the Patagonian Indians, while Ariel brings Prospero 'dew from the still-vex'd Bermoothes', or Bermuda.

In 1609 the Earl of Southampton sent a large fleet with the men and equipment necessary to colonize Virginia, the first English colony on the North American coast. The expedition raised hopes of fabulous fortunes and fired the imagination. For the first time not only astronomers, but also merchants, bankers and politicians realized that the earth is really round. The world inhabited by man was enlarged to twice its size in the course of a century. The discovery of another hemisphere caused a shock that can only be compared to the landing of an earth-launched rocket on the moon and the photographing of its farther side. . . .

Recent commentators connect the origins of *The Tempest* with the accounts of the English fleet's expedition to Virginia in 1609. The expedition failed. The flag-ship *Sea Adventure*, caught in a storm, was wrecked and the sailors landed on an uninhabited island, forming part of Bermuda. They spent ten months there; then they built two new ships and eventually managed to reach Virginia. They called the islands on which they were thrown by the storm, Devil's Islands. At night they could hear mysterious howls and noises, which – according to contemporary accounts – they attributed to demons. It is from them that Shakespeare may have taken the Boatswain's story of:

> strange and several noises
> Of roaring, shrieking, howling, jingling chains,
> And more diversity of sounds, all horrible.

(Act V, Sc. 1)

These accounts made the colonists indignant, and the council of the colonists of Virginia published a pamphlet by William Barrett declaring that rumours of Bermuda being visited by devils and evil spirits were false, or at any rate exaggerated, and that in the 'tragical comedy there is nothing that could discourage the colonists'.[2] The settlers of Virginia interpreted Shakespeare more sensibly than some of his most recent commentators.

It has also been found that Prospero fed Caliban with a certain kind of inedible 'fresh-brook mussels', mentioned in accounts of the unfortunate

108

expedition. In Ariel setting fire to the ship ('I'd divide, and burn in many places; on the topmast, the yards, and bowsprit, would I flame distinctly') some Shakespearian scholars see the picture of the St. Elmo fires, which so terrified those who were shipwrecked at the time of the Bermuda disaster.

Shakespeare's fantastic vision was always based on contemporary realities; thanks to them the world he showed in a condensed form on the stage became even more concrete. But it was always the whole world. It is useless, therefore, to look for the longitude and latitude of Prospero's island.

. . . In any event, *The Tempest* is a long way removed from the naive enthusiasm and childish pride of the first witnesses of geographical discoveries. The questions raised by *The Tempest* are philosophical and bitter.

The morality staged by Prospero will last less than four hours. But the island itself is outside time. There is on it both winter and summer. Prospero bids Ariel 'to run upon the sharp wind of the north, to do. . . business in the veins o'the earth when it is bak'd with frost'. The island has salt and sweet waters, barren and fertile lands, lemon groves and quagmires. It abounds in hazel-nuts, apples are ripe, there are truffles in the forest. The island is inhabited by baboons, hedgehogs, vipers, bats and toads. Jays have their nests here, sea-gulls perch on the rocks. Berries grow here, there are sea-shells of various kinds; feet are hurt by thorns; one hears mastiffs bark and cocks crow.

Commentators on *The Tempest* find on this island the idyllic atmosphere of an Arcadia. No doubt they interpret the play only through bad theatre performances; those with a ballet-dancer and a translucent screen. They see fairy-tale and ballet all the time. Well, one would rather trust those who undergo on this island the trial of madness:

> All torment, trouble, wonder, and amazement,
> Inhabit here: some heavenly power guide us
> Out of this fearful country!

> (Act V, Sc. 1)

That is why it is useless to look for Prospero's island even among the white spaces of old maps, where the contours of the land grow indistinct, the ocean blue turns pale and either drawings of fantastic monsters appear, or the inscription: *ubi leones*. Even there the island does not exist. Prospero's island is either the world, or the stage. To the Elizabethans it was all the same; the stage was the world, and the world was the stage.

On Prospero's island, Shakespeare's history of the world is played out, in an abbreviated form. It consists of a struggle for power, murder, revolt and violence. The first two acts of that history had been played out even before the arrival of Alonso's ship. Now Prospero will speed up the action. Twice more will the same history be repeated; as a tragedy, and as a grotesque; then the performance will be over. Prospero's island has nothing in common with the happy isles of Renaissance utopias. It rather reminds us of the islands in the world of the late Gothic. Such worlds were painted by one of the greatest visionaries among painters, precursor of the Baroque and Surrealism, the mad Hieronymus Bosch. They rise out of a grey sea. They are brown or yellow.

109

They take the form of a cone, reminding one of a volcano, with a flat top. On such hills tiny human figures swarm and writhe like ants. The scenes depict the seven deadly sins and the human passions, above all lechery and murder, drunkenness and gluttony. As well as people there are demons with beautiful, slender angelic female bodies and toads' or dogs' heads. Under the tables shaped like big tortoise-shells, old hags with flabby breasts and children's faces lie embracing half-men, half-insects with long hairy spider-like feet. Tables are set for a common feast, but the jugs and plates assume the shape of insects, birds or frogs. This island is a garden of torment, or a picture of mankind's folly. It is even similar in its shape to the Elizabethan stage. Boats arrive at a quiet harbour at the foot of the mountain. This is the apron-stage. The main scenes take place in large caves and on terraces of the volcanic cone. The flat top of the mountain is empty. There are no actors on the upper stage. No one gives his blessing or sits in judgement over the follies depicted. The island is the scene of the world's cruel tortures. In that world Shakespeare was a witness. But there are no gods in it, and gods are not needed. Men will suffice:

> Our natures do pursue,
> Like rats that ravin down their proper bane,
> A thirsty evil; and when we drink we die.

(Act I, Sc. 2)

This quotation from *Measure for Measure* could serve as an inscription to the large canvases by Bosch depicting *The Temptation of St. Anthony* or *The Garden of Pleasure*. Such is Prospero's island. Ariel is its angel and its executioner. That is why when wishing to be seen he assumes in turn the form of a nymph and a harpy. This is the sentence he pronounces on the ship-wrecked:

> Destiny, –
> That hath to instrument this lower world
> And what is in't, – the never-surfeited sea
> Hath caus'd to belch up you; and on this island,
> Where man doth not inhabit, – you 'mongst men
> Being most unfit to live. I have made you mad;
> And even with such-like valour men hang and drown
> Their proper selves.

(Act III, Sc. 3)

On Prospero's orders Ariel pursues the shipwrecked, leads them astray by his music, torments and scatters them. Alonso, the King of Naples, and the loyal Gonzalo are tired. They fall asleep with the entire retinue. Only the treacherous Antonio, and the King's brother, Sebastian, are to keep watch. The story of the plot aimed at seizing power will repeat itself. But Shakespeare uses a different mirror. The loss of the dukedom by Prospero has been told concisely, with a dry precision, as if in a history text-book; it has been unfolded like a formula, like a mechanism. This time, action is slowed down and shown in a typically Shakespearian close up – as in a film. Every second counts, and we can observe every vibration of the soul, every gesture. The King and Gonzalo are asleep. The moment is ripe. It may never happen again:

> *Sebastian.* But, for your conscience, –
> *Antonio.* Ay, sir; where lies that? if 'twere a kibe,
>   'Twould put me to my slipper; but I feel not
>   This deity in my bosom: twenty consciences,
>   That stand 'twixt me and Milan, candied be they,
>   And melt, ere they molest!

(Act II, Sc. 1)

Antonio and Sebastian raise their swords. In a moment murder will be committed. Shakespeare is, indeed, obsessed by this theme. Only the mirrors change. And every one of these mirrors is just another commentary on situations that remain the same. Prospero's island, like Denmark, is a prison. Antonio's and Sebastian's plot repeats scenes from *King Lear;*

> If that the heavens do not their visible spirits
> Send quickly down to tame these vile offences,
> It will come,
> Humanity must perforce prey on itself,
> Like monsters of the deep.

(Act IV, Sc. 2)

Swords will be put back again, for Ariel is watching. He is both an agent-provocateur and the stage-manager of the performance produced by Prospero. Murder does not have to be committed. It is enough that it has been exposed. for it is only a morality that is being performed on the island. Prospero submits the castaways to a trial of madness. But what does this madness mean? Sebastian repeats Antonio's deed of twelve years ago. The island is a stage on which the history of the world is being acted and repeated. History itself is madness. . . .

Prospero conducts his characters through ultimate, eschatological situations. Sebastian repeats Antonio's attempt to assassinate his brother and gain power. But Antonio had made his attempt in Milan in order to become a real duke. Sebastian wants to murder his king and brother on a desert island. The ship has been tossed on the rocks, and only a handful of survivors are left stranded in a strange land. Sebastian's attempt is in fact a disinterested act, pure folly; like the theft of a sack of gold in a desert, among people condemned to die of thirst. Sebastian's gestures and motives are identical with Antonio's gestures and motives of twelve years ago, following the pattern of a real *coup d'état.* This is the essence of Shakespearian analogy and of the system of ever-changing mirrors. The history of mankind is madness, but in order to expose it, one has to act it out on a desert island.

The first tragic sequence of the scenario devised by Prospero is over. The coup d'état has been performed. But it has been performed by princes. The law of analogy has not yet been exhausted, and another great confrontation awaits us. Actors and their parts are changed again, but the situation remains the same. Shakespeare's world is a unit, and a conglomeration not only of styles. A *coup d'état* is not the privilege of princes only; and it is not just the princes who have a passion for power. A coup d'état has already been shown in *The Tempest* three times through tragic lenses; now it will be performed as a buffoonery. Characters in the Shakespearian theatre are divided into tragic and grotesque. But grotesque in the Shakespearian theatre is not just a gay interlude, intended to entertain the audience after the cruel scenes performed by kings and dukes. Tragic scenes in Shakespeare often have *buffo,* grotesque, or ironic undertones and the *buffo* scenes are often mixed with bitterness, lyricism and cruelty. In his theatre it is the clowns who tell the truth. And not just tell it; they re-enact situations usually reserved for princes. Stephano, the drunkard, and Trinculo, the clown, want power too. Together with Caliban they organize an attempt on Prospero's life. History again repeats itself. But this time it is only a farce. This farce, too, will prove itself tragic. But for the moment it is pure buffoonery:

> Monster, I will kill this man: his daughter and I will
> be king and queen, – save our graces! – and Trinculo
> and thyself shall be viceroys.

(Act III, Sc. 2)

Prospero's island is a scene symbolizing the real world, not a utopia. Shakespeare explains this clearly when speaking directly to the audience, almost over-emphatically. Gonzalo is the reasoner of the drama. He is loyal and honest, but simple-minded and ridiculous at the same time. The King has not yet fallen asleep. The assassination has not yet been attempted. Gonzalo begins to tell a story of a happy country. He must have read recently the famous chapter on cannibals from Montaigne's *Essays*. He is repeating Montaigne's words. In that happy country work and commerce are unknown, there are no offices and no power:

> *Gonzalo (ending).* No sovereignty, – . . .
> *Antonio.* The latter end of his commonwealth forgets the
> beginning.
> *Gonzalo.* All things in common nature should produce
> Without sweat or endeavour: treason, felony,
> Sword, pike, knife, gun, or need or any engine,
> Would I not have; but nature should bring forth,
> Of it own kind, all foison, all abundance,
> To feed my innocent people.

(Act II, Sc. 1)

Human beings, beautiful and intelligent, live in a state of nature, free from original sin and uncorrupted by civilization. Nature is good and people are good. Such are the happy isles of the anti-feudal utopias. They were being discovered in the South Seas by the simple friars of the Order of St. Francis

112

who found in them – long before Rousseau – good and noble savages. These 'noble savages' had been written about by Montaigne. But Shakespeare did not believe in 'good savages', just as he did not believe in 'good kings'. When he did look for a Utopia, he located it in the forest of Arden, where Robin Hood had been with his company. But even this utopia had an element of bitterness in it: Jaques did not find his place even there. Shakespeare did not believe in the happy isles. They were too close to the known continents. . . .

On Prospero's island the laws of the real world apply to an even higher degree than in the forest of Arden. No sooner has Gonzalo finished telling his story and lain down to sleep beside the King than Antonio and Sebastian stand over him, bare swords in hand. A show commences, as cruel as the world; the same world that Hamlet looked upon:

> . . . the whips and scorns of time,
> The oppressor's wrong, the proud man's contumely,
> The pangs of despised love, the law's delay,
> The insolence of office, and the spurns
> That patient merit of the unworthy takes . . .
>
> (*Hamlet*, Act III, Sc. 1)

Ariel has fulfilled Prospero's orders. His enemies have repeated gestures of twelve years ago. Gestures, not deeds. From the first to the final scene they were just a handful of shipwrecked men on a desert island. In such a situation they could only repeat naive gestures. These gestures were madness itself, and this is the essence of the trial through which Prospero leads his actors. They have gone the whole way to the hell raging in their own souls. They have at last seen themselves 'naked like worms'. This expression taken from Sartre fits here most aptly. Alonso has realized the purpose of this trial:

> This is as strange a maze as e'er men trod;
> And there is in this business more than nature
> Was ever conduct of . . .
>
> (Act V, Sc. 1)

The performance of *The Tempest* and the morality produced by Prospero is drawing to an end. It is almost six o'clock. The same clock has counted the inner time of the performance and, the time of the audience. For it is both actors and spectators who – in the course of four hours – have gone through the same tempest. Everybody, in fact.

> Not a soul
> But felt a fever of the mad, and play'd
> Some tricks of desperation.
>
> (Act I, Sc. 2)

On the island, which Shakespearian scholars took to be Arcadia, the history of the world has once more been performed and repeated.

Notes

1. Analogy as a principle of Shakespeare's dramatic writing has been referred to by F. Fergusson, *The Idea of a Theatre* (Princeton, 1949); R. Moulton, *Shakespeare as a Dramatic Artist* (Oxford, 1885); W. Empson, *Some Versions of Pastoral* (1935). Henry James uses the term 'the central reflector' in connection with *Hamlet*.

2. Quoted by L. Chambrun, *Shakespeare Retrouvé* (1947).

Review Questions & Answers

Question 1.

The Tempest has been described as a specimen of purely romantic drama. Why is it not a tragedy or a comedy?

Answer

Bearing in mind that to instruct delightfully is the general end of all poetry, we may make a distinction between tragedy and comedy as follows:–

A *Tragedy* is a dramatic representation of a serious action, which must either be true, or at least have a likeness of truth, and which, by moving fear and pity, is conducive to the rectifying or purging of those two passions in our minds. The action of a tragedy must have order in it; that is, it must have a natural beginning, middle, and an end, every incident arising naturally out of a preceding incident. Tragedy deals with great actions such as murders, wars, depositions; and blind passions and stubborn strength of will generally characterize the principal actors in it. In tragedy the dramatist excites our fear by setting before our eyes some terrible example of misfortune which happened to persons of unusual strength of character or in high position in life, and our pity is moved when we see that the most virtuous as well as the greatest are not exempt from such misfortunes.

A *Comedy* is a dramatic representation of the lighter faults of mankind, with an intention to make vice and folly ridiculous. The follies and weaknesses which in comedy are usually made to appear contemptible are such as selfishness and egotism, vanity, dullness, pedantry, hypocrisy, and deceit. The scene must not, in this form of the drama, lie in heroic, warlike times, as in tragedy, but in the domestic circle; while the characters, instead of being kings, princes, warriors, or patriots, generally belong to a middle station in life.

The Tempest belongs to a special form of drama, in which there is a blending of tragedy and comedy, the play possessing the serious turn of the tragedy and the cheerful conclusion of the comedy. It includes tragic characters, with strong passions, but either they are endowed with a self-command which does not give up to passion, as in the case of Prospero, or the threatenings of fate are disarmed by a kind of overruling Providence (personified by Prospero), as in the case of the conspirators.

There is a romantic element about the incidents of the play, and a picturesque romantic background of sea and island landscape. We may feel a sympathetic pity for the sufferers, but our passions are not stirred; and though we read the play with feelings of contentment and pleasure, we are not moved to loud laughter, nor kept in a state of prolonged merriment. For these reasons *The Tempest* may be described as a specimen of purely romantic drama.

Question 2.

What are the leading features in the character of Prospero? Illustrate your answer by quotations.

Answer

In our consideration of the leading features of Prospero's character we will, for the sake of convenience, regard him under two different aspects – as a man and a father, and as a magician and ruler.

PROSPERO AS A MAN AND A FATHER

Prospero, although a magician, is at the same time human; and being susceptible to all the passions and emotions of a man, and subject to the same temptations and trials, he may be regarded from exactly the same points of view from which we criticize our fellow-creatures. Viewing him under this aspect, we shall see that Shakespeare has not committed the error of attempting to delineate a perfect man, and that Prospero has his failings; that he was neither absolutely just, nor infallibly wise, nor exempt from moments of petulance and irritability. But his human weaknesses only serve to show wherein his real strength lay – in his self-mastery, his capacity for learning wisdom by experience, his disinterestedness of soul, his forgiving nature, love, and sympathy.

His affection for his daughter and for his friends. – His love for Miranda was boundless. All his toils and labors were directed to the promotion of her welfare.

> "I have done nothing but in care of thee;
> Of thee, my dear one; thee, my daughter."

His love for her gave him strength to endure.

> "O, a cherubim
> Thou wast that did preserve me . . .
> raised in me
> An undergoing stomach, to bear up
> Against what should ensue."

In the desert island he watched tenderly over her education. To him she was "a loved darling," "dear heart," and "a rich gift," one who

> "will outstrip all praise,
> And make it halt behind her."

He experienced the greatest joy of his life when he saw that success had crowned his endeavors to bring about an attachment between Ferdinand and Miranda.

115

> "It goes on, I see,
> As my soul prompts it. Spirit, fine spirit! I'll free thee
> Within two days for this."

And again,

> "So glad of this as they I cannot be,
> Who are surprised withal; but my rejoicing
> At nothing can be more."

Next to his daughter, herself the "third of his own life or that for which he lived," of all the world he loved his brother Antonio, until his perfidy drove him from Milan. Many passages in the play testify to his affection for "the good old lord Gonzalo," whose honor, he says, "cannot be measured or confined." He sheds tears of joy and gratitude on meeting him.

> "Holy Gonzalo, honorable man,
> Mine eyes, even sociable to the show of thine,
> Fall fellowy drops."

and declares that his loyalty shall be rewarded both in word and deed. Not less is the love he feels towards Ferdinand, for all his apparent harshness; while his attitude towards Ariel is that of an affectionate parent towards a mischievous, frolicsome, yet beloved child.

He is a profound student. By his love of study he was the innocent cause of his misfortunes. As duke of Milan he was esteemed "for the liberal arts without a parallel." While dedicating himself to closeness and to the bettering of his mind, he neglected his duties to his state. In his narration to his daughter, he says

> "The government I cast upon my brother,
> And to my state grew stranger, being transported
> And rapt in secret studies."

But the knowledge thus gained was not destined to be wasted even from a material point of view, for his profound science afterwards became the source of his power and influence over the spiritual world.

He is of a generous, trustful disposition. Unlimited confidence in the virtue of others characterized his earlier years; generosity, tempered by the discretion that experience teaches, his later. His boundless trust in his brother Antonio

> "did beget of him
> A falsehood in its contrary as great
> As his trust was; which had indeed no limit."

And when first he came to the island he used Caliban, "filth as he was," with human care; pitied him, taught him each hour one thing or other, until he showed his gratitude by attempting to violate the honor and purity of his daughter. In the end Prospero forgives all his enemies, even his unnatural brother.

116

>"For you most wicked sir, whom to call brother
>Would even infect my mouth, I do forgive
>Thy rankest fault; all of them."

He has learnt now to recognize sincere repentance, and he knows how much "the rarer action is in virtue than in vengeance."

He is subject to occasional fits of irritability. This characteristic we mention only to show that he is human, and that in his solitude he had developed his powers of subduing any unworthy passions that might temporarily assail him. Were we not permitted occasional glimpses of Prospero's sensitiveness, we could not fully appreciate his highly developed will. By his "nobler reason," he rises superior to the natural instinct of revenge, and controls himself in moments of excitability and fury. When Miranda opposes him, he seems to exert his paternal authority with unnecessary harshness. "Silence!" he says; "one word more shall make me chide thee, if not hate thee." When the time came for the accomplishment of the drunkards' plot he is violently moved.

>"Your father's in some passion
>That works him strongly."

says Ferdinand to his betrothed, who replies that never in all her experience of him had she seen him "touch'd with anger so distemper'd." Prospero is aware of his weakness, for which he asks Ferdinand's indulgence.

>"Sir, I am vex'd;
>Bear with my weakness; my old brain is troubled;
>Be not disturb'd with my infirmity";

and he takes "a turn or two" to still his beating mind.

PROSPERO AS MAGICIAN AND RULER.

Prospero differs from most professors of magic of whom we have read in the extent of his power and in the absolute purity of his motives. As he had no other object in view than that of facilitating the march of retributive justice, his practice of magic never seems to us to be, what it really was, the fulfilling of an unlawful contract with the devil. There is such grandeur and such dignity in all his actions, that he appears rather as a beneficent Providence than as an enchanter in league with the powers of hell.

Scientific knowledge is the foundation of his skill. He repeatedly alludes to his books, which he says he prizes above his dukedom.

>"I'll to my book,
>For yet ere supper-time must I perform
>Much business appertaining."

Caliban was aware of their value to the magician. "Burn but his books," says he.

>"for without them
>He's but a sot, as I am, nor hath not
>One spirit to command."

117

His relations towards his spiritual agents. The service of a magician's spirits was voluntary, so that the readiness with which Prospero was served bears witness to the moderation and mercy with which he exerted his powers. Not only did he command the respect of all his servants, but in the case of Ariel he even inspired love and affection and sympathy with sorrow. More than once he commends his faithful messenger and his "meaner ministers" for the worthy performance of their tasks. That he could be severe, and knew how to enforce obedience when necessary is evident from all his dealings with Caliban.

His power was almost unlimited. That his art was in the highest degree potent appears by his authoritative address, commencing "Ye elves of hills, brooks, standing lakes, and groves." Caliban confesses that

> "his art is of such power,
> It would control my dam's god, Setebos,
> And make a vassal of him."

The most striking testimony to his power is the faithfulness of his attendant sprite Ariel, for it was given only to the most powerful of magicians to exercise authority over spirits resident in the highest regions of spiritual existence. Sycorax could inflict punishment upon the delicate spirit, but could not again undo the torment.

Prospero as a Ruler. As ruler and prince over his spiritual subjects, Prospero shows how amply he had made up for his early neglect in Milan. Now he is the stern, yet just disciplinarian, ruling with a firm hand, respected and even feared by his subjects. He is conscious of his power, and he knows, too, how much of it is due to magic, and how much to his own strength of character. He pardons his enemies, because he feels that by his moral character he is raised far above their capacity to injure him. With a lofty magnanimity, almost suggesting disdain, he forgives them, declaring that,

> "they being penitent,
> The sole drift of my purpose doth extend
> Not a frown further."

Then with calm superiority, knowing how secure is his new hold upon his old enemies, he abjures his rough magic, breaks his staff, and drowns his book. Dignified and majestic as he nearly always is, he shows himself in nothing else so divinely grand as in the final scenes of the play. In the Epilogue, after having voluntarily divested himself of all his magic power, he, the pardoner, himself demands pardon, to remind us, perhaps, that the noblest and best of mortals has imperfections, and requires forgiveness. "Without my spirits," he says, "my ending is despair,

> Unless it be relieved by prayer.
> Which pierces so that it assaults
> Mercy itself, and frees all faults."

118

Question 3.

How do Miranda's first words indicate that the story of the play has in it something of the nature of a fairy tale?

Answer

From Miranda's first words, and from the subsequent speeches by which her father strives to subdue the alarm felt by her sympathetic nature, we learn that Prospero is an enchanter, a magician of great power and influence, and that the tempest and shipwreck were attributable to his magic arts. We are thus prepared for further flights into the realm of fairyland; nor have we long to wait before we make acquaintance. Ariel, the most important of Prospero's spiritual agents, and liveliest inhabitant of his enchanted isle.

Question 4.

Show that pity is a distinguishing virtue in Miranda's character.

Answer

We have already seen how Miranda's sympathy was evoked by the sight of the shipwrecked sufferers and by the narrative of her father's disasters; and now her father's unfriendly treatment of Ferdinand again excites her pity. She implores her father not to make too rash a trial of him; she hangs upon his garments, endures stern rebuke, and offers to become surety for her lover, who must be innocent, she feels, for "there's nothing ill can dwell in such a temple"; and lastly, contrives to whisper sweet and comforting words in Ferdinand's ear, that will make his labors pleasures and odious drudgery a sport. Her father's last words, "Speak not for him", are spoken in answer to her piteous, beseeching look.

Question 5.

What different parts of human nature are typified in the inhabitants of the island?

Answer

Various are the allegorical significances which have been ascribed to the different inhabitants of the island. Prospero is said to be the embodiment of Imagination, Ariel of Fancy, Caliban of brute Understanding, Miranda of abstract Womanhood, Ferdinand of Youth, compelled to learn the nobility of self-sacrifice and the gospel of work. Or, again, Prospero is a type of the Artist's or Creative Genius, Miranda of Art in its infancy, Caliban of the grosser Passions, and Ariel of the imaginative genius of Poetry.

Question 6.

In what different shapes and for what purposes did Ariel appear?

Answer

Ariel enters upon the scene on seventeen occasions. On eight of these occasions he is "invisible" – i.e., invisible to all eyes except those of Prospero. On seven occasions he is present upon the stage with Prospero alone, and we have no indication as to what shape he then assumed, but we may reasonably presume that he was invisible to the same extent as before. Once he enters "like a water-nymph," and in this shape he appears "a fine apparition." At another time he enters amid thunder and lightning "like a harpy," with wings which he can clap; this figure, too, he "bravely performed," so that "a grace it had, devouring." Although his entrance is not denoted in the first scene of the play, yet he was present during the shipwreck in the form of a meteor, or a supernatural light darting from masts to rigging, from yards to bowsprit, dividing in twain, and anon meeting and joining again.

Generally, Ariel enters for the purpose of receiving Prospero's commands, and departs to execute them, or else we find him actually engaged in the performance of his master's behests. Sometimes he employs music as a means of leading the actors from one spot to another, as in the cases of Ferdinand, Stephano, and Trinculo. He uses the same means to lull to sleep the weary travellers (Act II, Sc. 1, 191) and a timely song in Gonzalo's ears saves the slumberer from the assassin's sword. The tricksy spirit takes pleasure more than once in befooling the drunken plotters, and, with Prospero, he takes part in inflicting condign punishment upon them. He brings upon the scene the actors in the visionary masque, and his last office is to find "calm seas and auspicious gales" to waft the royal fleet to Naples.

Question 7.

Give an account of the two conspiracies mentioned in the play, showing their points of contrast and resemblance.

Answer

The conspiracy of Caliban and his associates against Prospero is a burlesque imitation of the conspiracy of Antonio and Sebastian against the King of Naples. In each case we have a dependent striving to free himself from the bondage to which he is subjected, and in each case the plot is frustrated by the providential foresight of Prospero and by the immediate agency of his servant Ariel.

In the first conspiracy Antonio and Sebastian attempt to kill Alonso and Gonzalo. Their opportunity presents itself unsought for. The intended victims are asleep on the ground, "no better than the earth they lie upon." Three inches of steel "can lay to bed for ever" the King of Naples and Gonzalo, and thus secure a kingdom to Sebastian and exemption from tribute to Antonio. Antonio is throughout the greater sinner, for, although he had least to gain by success, it was he who devised the plot, roused the more torpid spirit of Sebastian to the necessary pitch of ambition, and held on his course in spite of his first failure, until they both found themselves caught in the meshes of Prospero's far-reaching net. When Prospero charged them with their crime and pardoned them, they showed no signs either of remorse or gratitude, but remained defiant and sullen to the end.

In the other conspiracy, Caliban, the subject, aims at freedom from bondage, and offers to the drunken butler, Stephano, the sovereignty of the island, which he holds to be his own by right. Here, then, as before, he who is to benefit least is the prompter and the moving spirit. Temptation is put in Caliban's way by the unexpected presence in the island of two fitting associates in crime. But there are difficulties to be surmounted, and courage is needed more than the coward monster can inspire them with. They nerve themselves with wine, and then, "red-hot with drinking," bend unswervingly towards their project. The cause of their failure was quite as much their own ridiculous folly as Prospero's power, and thus rested with themselves more than it did in the case of the other conspirators. With the exception, perhaps of Caliban, they never seem to have taken themselves really seriously: and as their guilt was less than that of Antonio and Sebastian, so also their conduct after defeat was less unworthy, for they repented, and Caliban promised to be "wise hereafter, and seek for grace."

Question 8.

The unities are said to be observed in this drama. Explain fully the meaning of this statement.

Answer

According to the old classical rules of art, the whole action of a drama should be carried on without change of scene, should relate to a period of not more than twenty-four hours, and should deal with one general subject. These were called the unities of Place, Time, and Action respectively. Such were Aristotle's rules, the classical fetters imposed also upon the French drama, and acknowledged by Corneille and Racine, but they were too artificial and too limited to suit the genius of our poet. As Pope has truly said,

> "Great wits sometimes may gloriously offend,
> And rise to faults true critics dare not mend."

Except in the case of *The Tempest*, Shakespeare has invariably violated the laws of Place and Time, and generally also the law of Action. In this play, however, the unities are to a great extent observed. The scene of action is confined within the narrow limits of a small island, the time consumed in the occurrence of the events narrated is particularly stated not to reach four hours, and all subordinate incidents depend upon and contribute towards one strong concentrated interest.

Question 9.

Point out the difficulties involved in using the supernatural for dramatic purposes. To what extent has Shakespeare overcome them?

121

Answer

The supernatural, in fictitious composition, requires to be managed with considerable delicacy, and should in general be sparingly employed, for the marvellous loses its effect by being brought much into view, and our feelings of wonder or terror soon give way under the influence of that familiarity which begets contempt. Burke has commented that obscurity is necessary to make anything terrible, and remarks that no person "seems better to have understood the secret of heightening, or of setting terrible things in their strongest light, by the force of a judicious obscurity, than Milton." But Shakespeare in *The Tempest* is neither indistinct nor obscure. He has given real life-like pictures of creatures that never had any real existence; as has been said, he has made "the supernatural natural, the wonderful ordinary". He has managed the marvellous in such a manner that the greatest miracle appears to the reader to be nothing more than an ordinary event produced by the simplest means, and reason is never offended by the appearance of the supernatural. The shipwreck, the separation of Ferdinand from his companions, and of the princes from the rest of the crew, the sudden and mutual attraction of Ferdinand and Miranda, and many other incidents produced by Prospero's magic power, seem only to have been brought about by the natural concurrence of circumstances, so that "we might strike magic out of the play, and nature would remain." Herein, says Charles Lamb, "the great and little wits are differentiated; that if the latter wander ever so little from Nature or actual existence, they lose themselves and their readers. Their phantoms are lawless, their visions nightmares. . . . For the supernatural, or something superadded to what we know of Nature, they give you the plainly non-natural."

Question 10.

Who were Iris, Ceres, and Juno? Describe briefly the parts they severally play in the masque.

Answer

Iris was originally a personification of the rainbow, but she was afterwards converted into the swift messenger of the gods, the rainbow being, as it were, a bridge between earth and heaven. She here appears in the united characters of Juno's "watery arch and messenger".

Ceres was a daughter of Cronos and Rheo. Her name (the Greek form Demeter) signifies Mother Earth, and she is, therefore, an expression of the ancient conception of the earth-goddess, with a special reference to nature and human civilization. She was the patron of all those arts which are more or less intimately connected with agriculture, and which men first learned from her. As the "bountiful daughter of heaven", she invokes a blessing upon Ferdinand and Miranda. (110-117.)

Juno, sister and wife of Jupiter, and queen of heaven. As the special patroness of marriage, she was supposed to watch over its sanctity, to vouchsafe the blessing of children, and to protect women in childbirth. (106-9.) In art she is often represented with a peacock (74) or goose at her feet.

Bibliography

Allen, D. C., *William Shakespeare: The Tempest, Image and Meaning*. Johns Hopkins Press and Oxford University Press, 1960.

Brown, John R. *Shakespeare: The Tempest* (Studies in English Literature) Boston: Dynamic Learning Corporation, 1972.

Brown, Ivor, *Shakespeare in his Time*. Edinburgh: Thomas Nelson and Sons, Ltd., 1961.

Chambers, E. K. *William Shakespeare: A Study of Facts and Problems*. 2 vols. Oxford: Clarendon Press, 1930.

James, D. G., *The Dream of Prospero*. Oxford: Clarendon Press, 1967.

Knight, G. W., *The Shakespearian Tempest*. Oxford University Press, 1932.

Palmer, D. J., ed. *The Tempest: A Casebook*. Great Britain: Macmillan & Co. Ltd., 1968.

Smith, Hallett, ed. *Twentieth Century Interpretations of the Tempest*. Englewood Cliffs, N.J.: Prentice-Hall, 1969.

Still, Colin, *Shakespeare's Mystery Play: A Study of The Tempest*. London: Cecil Palmer, 1921.

Tobias, Richard C., and Zolbrod, Paul G., eds. *Shakespeare's Late Plays: Essays in Honor of Charles Crow*. Athens, Ohio: Ohio University Press, 1975.

Wilson, J. Dover, *The Essential Shakespeare: A Biographical Adventure*. Cambridge: University Press, 1933.

_____. *The Meaning of The Tempest*. Published by the Literary and Philosophical Society of Newcastle upon Tyne, 1936.

NOTES